THE NORTH AND THE SOUTH:

BEING A

STATISTICAL VIEW

OF THE CONDITION OF THE

FREE AND SLAVE STATES.

BY

HENRY CHASE AND C. H. SANBORN.

Compiled from Official Documents.

PUBLISHED … MPANY

CLEVELAND, OHIO:

HENRY P. B. JEWETT.

1857

Republished 1972

Scholarly Press, Inc., 22929 Industrial Drive East

St. Clair Shores, Michigan 48080

Entered according to Act of Congress, in the year 1856, by

JOHN P. JEWETT AND COMPANY,

In the Clerk's Office of the District Court of the District of Massachusetts

Library of Congress Cataloging in Publication Data

Chase, Henry.
    The North and the South.

    Reprint of the 2d ed.
    1. United States--Statistics. I. Sanborn,
Charles Henry, 1822-1899, joint author. II. Title.
E431.C48 1972   317.3   75-116280
ISBN 0-403-00437-3

PREFACE.

It is the object of this work to compare the condition of the slaveholding and non-slaveholding States—the North and the South—as to territory, population, industry and wealth, education and intelligence, religion and moral advancement, and general progress. The authorities used are the official documents of the General Government and of the individual States. The calculations are, for the most part, for the year 1850, and based on the census returns for that year, as compiled by J. D. B. De Bow, and published in his Compendium of the Seventh Census.

. This work, prepared with much labor, is the only one of the kind within our knowledge. We think there is public necessity for it, and submit it without further remark.

Concord, Mass., September, 1856.

CONTENTS.

(iv)

INTRODUCTORY.

THE slaveholding States, fifteen in number, including the semi-slave States of Delaware and Maryland, have an area of eight hundred and fifty-one thousand, four hundred and forty-eight square miles. In latitude, they extend from 25° to 40° north, and, in longitude, from 75° to 107° west. This vast empire of nearly a thousand miles square has a sea and gulf coast of seven thousand miles in extent, and is drained by more than fifty navigable rivers. Through its centre flows the longest river of the globe, with its thousands of miles of navigable waters.

The free States, sixteen in number, have an area of six hundred and twelve thousand five hundred and ninety-seven square miles. Exclusive of California, they extend, in latitude, from 37° to 47° north, and, in longitude, from 67° to 97° west. With California, they constitute a territory of nearly eight hundred miles square, with two thousand miles of Atlantic seacoast. A dozen navigable rivers flow from this territory to the Atlantic, two of them finding a passage to the sea through the far-extending bays of the slave States. By the great lakes and their outlets, its northern products find their natural channel to the ocean — ice-bound for several months in the year — through the territory of a foreign power; while, borne on the Mississippi for more than a thousand miles through the domain of slavery, its western products seek a passage to the ocean by the Gulf of Mexico. . While the rivers of the slave States are never closed to navigation by the rigors of climate, those of the free States are closed by ice during the winter months of each year.

In climate, the slave States excel, and in soil equal, the free. Certain productions, moreover, of great importance are mostly confined, by the laws of temperature, to the slave States. Among these are cotton, cane-sugar, rice, and tobacco.

Thus, for agriculture, the slave States have a fertile soil, a climate

1*

(v)

adapted to the productions of tropical and temperate latitudes; for manufactures, an exhaustless motive power distributed throughout its whole extent, with the raw materials of cotton, wool, iron, lumber, etc., abundant and readily accessible, while coal, salt, and other precious metals are found in several of these States; for internal commerce, numerous rivers draining the whole territory; for external commerce, thousands of miles of sea and gulf coast with excellent harbors.

The rigorous climate of all, and the sterile soil of some of the free States, render them less fitted for agriculture than the slave States, while the transportation of the raw material affects the success of manufactures. For the purposes of commerce, the North has a moderate extent of seacoast and several good harbors, whose remoteness, however, from the producing and consuming regions affect disadvantageously the interests of trade. The great lakes, when not closed by ice, furnish good facilities for internal commerce.

In the origin of their population and the date of their settlement, the North and the South are pretty nearly alike.

Geographically, it will be seen that the old and new free States are nearly separated by the projection of Canada and northern Virginia, while the Pacific State of California is separated from the other free States by two thousand miles of unsettled country. The slave States, old and new, on the other hand, lie in a compact body. Resulting from these different geographical positions were the facts that the emigration from the older free States must seek, by extended and circuitous routes, a passage to the new; while the emigration from the slave States had only to cross a border line, of a thousand miles in extent, to find itself at once on its new territory.

THE NORTH AND THE SOUTH.

CHAPTER I.

TERRITORY.

As the basis for future comparisons, in this work, the following table is introduced, showing the area of the several States, together with that of the two great sections, the North and the South:

TABLE I.

Showing the Area of the Slave and the Free States.

SLAVE STATES.	Area in Sq. Miles.	FREE STATES.	Area in Sq. Miles.
Alabama................	50,722	California	155,980
Arkansas	52,198	Connecticut...........	4,674
Delaware	2,120	Illinois	55,405
Florida	59,268	Indiana	33,809
Georgia................	58,000	Iowa...................	50,914
Kentucky	37,680	Maine..................	31,766
Louisiana	41,255	Massachusetts	7,800
Maryland	11,124	Michigan	56,243
Mississippi	47,156	New Hampshire........	9,280
Missouri	67,380	New York	47,000
North Carolina	50,704	New Jersey	8,320
South Carolina	29,385	Ohio	39,964
Tennessee..............	45,600	Pennsylvania	46,000
Texas	237,504	Rhode Island	1,306
Virginia	61,352	Vermont	10,212
....	......	Wisconsin	53,924
Total..................	851,448	Total	612,597

It will be seen by the above table that the area of the fifteen slaveholding States is 851,448 square miles; and that of the sixteen non-slaveholding States 612,597 square miles; a difference of more than 238,000 square miles in favor of the Slave States.*   Let it be remembered, therefore, that the area of the Free States is considerably less than three-fourths that of the Slave States.

By the purchase of Louisiana, in 1803, and of Florida, in 1819, were added to the national domain 966,479 square miles; an area greater than the *entire area* of the United States at the time of gaining their independence.†   By the annexation of Texas, in 1846, were added 318,000 miles more, and by a treaty with Mexico at the close of the war, 522,955 square miles; making an aggregate of 1,807,434 square miles.   This, of course, is exclusive of the 308,052 square miles to which our title was "confirmed" by treaty with Great Britain in 1846.

The expense of these purchases and conquests cannot be exactly determined.   The territory of Louisiana, purchased of France, cost $15,000,000; that of Florida, purchased of Spain, $5,000,000; amount paid Texas, about $27,000,000; expenses of Mexican war, $217,175,575; paid for New Mexico, by treaty, $15,000,000.   Making an aggregate of more than $270,000,000, which, together with interest on the same, the expense of the Florida war, about $100,000,000, and nearly the same amount paid for the extinguishment of Indian titles, etc., etc., make a sum, little if any short of $1,000,000,000.

The manner in which this territory has been apportioned to the two sections is given by Mr. Clay, in his speech in the Senate in 1850.   (See *Appendix to Congress. Globe*, vol. 22, part 1, page 126.)

---

* The estimates here made are according to the *Compendium of the United States Census*.   In the Quarto Edition the area of Texas is given as 325,520 square miles; which would make the area of the Slave States nearly 100,000 square miles more than here given.

† See *Compendium United States Census*, p. 32.

He says: "What have been the territorial acquisitions made by this country, and to what interests have they conduced? Florida, where slavery exists, has been introduced. All the most valuable parts of Louisiana have also added to the extent and consideration of the slaveholding portion of the Union." .... "All Louisiana, with the exception of what lies north of 36° 30';" .... "all Texas, all the territories which have been acquired by the Government of the United States during sixty years of the operation of that Government, have been slave territories — theatres of slavery — with the exception I have mentioned lying north of the line of 36° 30'."

California has since been admitted a Free State. The other States, formed from territory thus obtained, and admitted into the Union, are Louisiana, Missouri, Arkansas, Florida, and Texas — five Slave States.

The area of California is 155,980 square miles; that of the five Slave States named, 457,605; being 302,625 square miles more, and very nearly in the ratio of three to one. Indeed, the area of these five purchased Slave States is greater than that of all the Free States, if we except California. It will be seen by tables VII and VIII, that the number of Representatives in Congress from California is two, which, together with two Senators, entitle that State to four electoral votes. The number of Representatives from the five Slave States is sixteen, which, together with ten Senators, make twenty-six electoral votes, being in the ratio of six and one-third to one, and a majority of twenty-two.

There is (of territory inhabited and uninhabited) north of the old Missouri Compromise line an area of 1,970,077 square miles, and 966,089 south of it.

It will be noticed, in passing, that the area of Virginia is not quite four thousand miles less than that of all New England, and is larger than that entire section if we except Connecticut. It is also larger than the four States of New York, Massachusetts, Connecticut, and Rhode Island. Maryland contains over three thousand square miles more than Massachusetts, and is considerably larger than either New Hampshire or Vermont; Pennsylvania and New York are each smaller than either North Carolina, Mississippi, Georgia, Arkansas, or Alabama; while Ohio and Indiana are still smaller. Ohio has but two thousand two hundred and eighty-four square miles more than Kentucky, to which it is very similar in surface, soil, and productions. South Carolina is almost four times as large as Massachusetts, and three-fourths as large as Ohio.

CHAPTER II.

POPULATION.

The following tables give the aggregate population of the several states in 1790, 1820, and 1850. (For a table showing the population at each decennial census, see *Appendix.*) In connection with this are also here given, the area, the number of inhabitants to a square mile in 1850, and the population at the present time, the last being taken from a late communication to Congress by the Secretary of the Treasury:

TABLE II.

Statement of the Area, and Aggregate Population in 1790, 1820, 1850, and 1856, with the Number of Inhabitants to a Square mile, in 1850, of the several Slave States.

SLAVE STATES.	Area in Sq.Miles.	Population in 1790.	Population in 1820.	Population in 1850.	Density in 1850.	Population in 1856
Alabama	50,722		127,901	771,623	15.21	835,192
Arkansas	52,198		14,273	209,897	4.02	253,117
Delaware	2,120	59,096	72,749	91,532	43.18	97,295
Florida........	59,268			87,445	1.48	110,725
Georgia	58,000	82,548	340,987	906,185	15.62	935,090
Kentucky......	37,680	73,077	564,317	982,405	26.07	1,086,587
Louisiana	41,255	319,728	153,407	517,762	12.55	600,387
Maryland	11,124		407,350	583,034	52.41	639,580
Mississippi.....	47,156		75,448	606,326	12.86	671,649
Missouri	67,380		66,586	682,044	10.12	831,215
North Carolina	50,704	393,751	638,829	869,039	17.14	921,852
South Carolina	29,385	249,073	502,741	668,507	22.75	705,661
Tennessee	45,600	35,791	422,813	1,002,717	21.99	1,092,470
Texas	237,504			212,592	0.89	500,000
Virginia.......	61,352	748,308	1,065,379	1,421,661	23.17	1,512,593
Total	851,448	1,961,372	4,452,780	9,612,769	11.28	10,793,413

TABLE III.

Statement of the Area, and Aggregate Population in 1790, 1820, 1850, *and* 1856, *with the Number of Inhabitants to a Square Mile, in* 1850, *of the several Free States.*

FREE STATES.	Area in Sq.Miles.	Population in 1790.	Population in 1820.	Population in 1850.	Density in 1850.	Population in 1856.
California	155,980			92,597	.59	335,000
Connecticut...	4,674	238,141	275,202	370,792	79.33	401,292
Illinois	55,405		55,211	851,470	15.37	1,242,917
Indiana	33,809		147,178	988,416	29.24	1,149,606
Iowa.........	50,914			192,214	3.78	325,014
Maine........	31,766	96,540	298,335	583,169	18.36	623,862
Massachusetts.	7,800	378,717	523,287	994,514	127.50	1,133,123
Michigan	56,243		8,896	397,654	7.07	509,374
New Hamps'ire	9,280	141,899	244,161	317,976	34.26	324,701
New York	47,000	340,120	1,372,812	3,097,394	65.90	3,470,059
New Jersey ...	8,320	184,139	277,575	489,555	58.84	569,499
Ohio .....:...	39,964		581,434	1,980,329	49.55	2,215,750
Pennsylvania .	46,000	434,373	1,049,458	2,311,786	50.26	2,542,960
Rhode Island .	1,306	69,110	83,059	147,545	112.97	166,927
Vermont	10,212	85,416	235,764	314,120	30.76	325,206
Wisconsin	53,924			305,391	5.66	552,109
Total	612,597	1,968,455	5,152,372	13,434,922	21.93	15,887,399

From these tables it will be seen that, in 1790, the population in the present non-slaveholding States was 1,968,455; and in the present slaveholding States, 1,961,372; showing a difference of 7,083 in favor of the non-slaveholding States. This difference, at first so slight, only 7,000, we find constantly increasing, until in 1820 (thirty years from that time) it becomes 699,592; the population of the slaveholding States being at that time 4,452,780, and that of the non-slaveholding States 5,152,372. In thirty years more (1850), the population of the fifteen Slave States is 9,612,769, and of the sixteen Free States 13,434,922; a difference of 3,822,153 in favor of the Free States. Thus, from having a majority of less than four-tenths of one per cent in 1790, the Free States had in

1850 a majority of more than thirty-nine per cent. And this, notwithstanding 87,000 inhabitants were added to the Slave States by the annexation of Louisiana and Florida, and a large population by the annexation of Texas.

The average number of inhabitants to a square mile, in the Slave States, is 11.28, and in the Free States 21.93; almost exactly two to one.

On examining this table a little in detail, we notice the following, among many other interesting facts:

The area of Virginia is 61,352 miles; that of New York is 47,000, or over 14,000 square miles less than that of Virginia. The population of Virginia, in 1790, was 748,308, and in 1850 it was 1,421,661. It had not doubled in sixty years. The population of New York in 1790 was 340,120, in 1850 it was 3,097,394; thus, New York had multiplied her population more than nine times in the same period. Kentucky has an area of 37,680 square miles, and Ohio 39,964, a little over two thousand miles greater. Kentucky had in 1850 a population of 982,405, and Ohio 1,980,329, or nearly a million more than Kentucky. Kentucky was admitted into the Union in 1792, and Ohio in 1802. The area of Mississippi is 47,156 square miles, that of Pennsylvania, 46,000. The population of Mississippi was, in 1850 (in round numbers), 606,000, that of Pennsylvania, 2,300,000. The number of inhabitants to a square mile in North Carolina was, in 1850, a little over seventeen, and in New Hampshire thirty-four; in Tennessee twenty-one, and in Ohio forty-nine; in South Carolina twenty-two, and in Massachusetts one hundred and twenty-seven.

These comparisons are based upon the population as it was in 1850. The tables likewise show the present population, as given in a recent communication to Congress, by the Secretary of the Treasury. By this it will be seen that the ratio of increase still continues; there being now a majority of 5,093,986 or over forty-seven per cent, in favor of the Free States

2

According to the same ratio, in less than three years more than two-thirds of the entire population of the Union will be found in the Free States.

The entire white population of the two sections, at each decennial census, from 1790 to 1850, is as follows (for a statement of white population at each census, see *Appendix*) :

Slaveholding States.		Non-slaveholding States.	
In 1790.	1,271,488	In 1790	1,900,976
1800	1,692,914	1800	2,601,509
1810	2,192,706	1810	3,653,219
1820	2,808,946	1820	5,030,377
1830	3,633,195	1830	6,871,302
1840	4,601,873	1840	9,557,065
1850	6,184,477	1850	13,238,670

The difference of increase here may perhaps seem more remarkable than in the aggregate population. The white population of the present Slave States was, in 1790, 1,271,448, and of the present non-slaveholding States, at the same time, 1,900,976, a difference of 629,488 ; not quite fifty per cent. in favor of the non-slaveholding states. In 1850 that difference had become 7,054,193, or over one hundred and fourteen per cent. In other words, the white population in the Free States had become 869,716 *more than double* that in the Slave States. The population of the latter being 6,184,477, and that of the former 13,238,670.

How far this difference, both of population and its increase, in the two sections, is due to foreign immigration, may be seen from the following statement (*Census Compendium*, p. 45) : " There are now 726,450 persons living in slaveholding States, who are natives of non-slaveholding States, and 232,112 persons living in non-slaveholding States, who are natives of slaveholding States. There are 1,866,397 persons of foreign birth in

the non-slaveholding States, and 378,205 in the slaveholding."
There are then 494,338 more natives of non-slaveholding
States in slaveholding States, than there are of slaveholding
in the non-slaveholding States; while there are 1,488,192 more
persons of foreign birth in the non-slaveholding than in the
slaveholding States; which gives less than a million more persons residing in non-slaveholding States, who were not born
there, than in the slaveholding States, nearly all of whom are
white inhabitants. The difference is nearly 4,000,000 in the
aggregate, and more than 7,000,000 in the white population,
and is not therefore due to *this* cause.

The following tables show the white population of the
several States in 1790, 1820, and 1850:

TABLE IV.

White Population of the Slave States in 1790, 1820, and 1850.

SLAVE STATES.	1790.	1820.	1850.
Alabama		85,451	426,514
Arkansas		12,579	162,189
Delaware	46,310	55,282	71,169
Florida			47,203
Georgia	52,886	189,566	521,572
Kentucky	61,133	434,644	761,413
Louisana		73,383	255,491
Maryland	208,649	260,223	417,943
Mississippi		42,176	295,718
Missouri		55,988	592,004
North Carolina	288,204	419,200	553,028
South Carolina	140,178	237,440	274,563
Tennessee	32,013	339,927	756,836
Texas			154,034
Virginia	442,115	603,087	894,800
Total	1,271,488	2,808,946	6,184,477

TABLE V

White Population of the Free States in 1790, 1820, *and* 1850.

FREE STATES.	1790	1820	1850
California			91,635
Connecticut	232,581	267,161	363,099
Illinois		53,788	846,034
Indiana.......................		145,758	977,154
Iowa..........................			191,881
Maine.........................	96,002	297,340	581,813
Massachusetts	373,254	516,419	985,450
Michigan		8,591	395,071
New Hampshire	141,111	243,236	317,456
New Jersey	169,954	257,409	465,509
New York	314,142	1,332,744	3,048,325
Ohio		576,572	1,955,050
Pennsylvania	424,099	1,017,094	2,258,160
Rhode Island..................	64,689	79,413	143,875
Vermont......................	85,144	234,846	313,402
Wisconsin			304,756
Total........................	1,900,976	5,030,377	13,238,670

The whole number of slaveholders in the Slave States, in 1850, was 346,048; and of this number 173,204 hold less than five slaves each, leaving 172,844 who are holders of more than four slaves; and, if we deduct the numbers holding less than ten slaves each, there will remain 92,215. The whole number of slaveholders, then, is less than 350,000, including females and minors. The number of voters in this class is therefore much smaller. But, counting them all as voters, they are less than the number of freemen who voted at the last Presidential election in New England, even without including Vermont. They are less than the number who voted in either Pennsylvania or Ohio, and less than two-thirds the number who voted in New York.

The annexed table shows the free colored population of the United States. It will be seen that the number of free colored inhabitants in the Free States is 196,016, and in the Slave States

2*

228,128, mingled with a white population of less than half that of the Free States. This, of course, does not include the District of Columbia, in which there are over 10,000 free colored persons; while the number in the Free States includes those in New Jersey, in which there are over 23,000, of whom 20,000 were born in the State. Indeed, if we examine the table giving the nativities of the free colored persons, we shall see that the number who still reside in the States where they were born is 354,470, out of the whole number, 454,495, which is over eighty-one per cent.

On page 81 of the *Census Compendium*, in connection with a table showing the occupation of the free colored males over fifteen years of age, it is stated that in New York city there is one in fifty-five engaged in pursuits requiring education; while in New Orleans one in eleven is engaged in similar pursuits. In Connecticut, one in a hundred is thus employed, and in Louisiana one in twelve.

These are the only cities and States compared in this way in the Census. It may be a fact a little surprising to some, that, while the ratio of the free colored inhabitants engaged in pursuits requiring education in Louisiana is one-twelfth of the whole, the ratio of the entire white male population engaged in the pursuits in the same State is less than one-eighteenth of the whole.

The increase in the present slaveholding States, from 1840 to 1850, is 10.49 per cent., and in the non-slaveholding States 14.98 per cent.; being four and a half per cent. greater in the Free than in the Slave States. The proportion of free colored persons to the total population, in some of the States, is quite considerable; being greatest in Maryland and Delaware, — in the former twelve, and in the latter nineteen per cent.

Had we not the example of De Bow's Compendium, we might be uncertain how to regard the slaves, whether as men,

TABLE VI.

Free Colored Population of the United States in the years 1790, 1820, 1850

SLAVE STATES.	1790	1820	1850	FREE STATES.	1790	1820	1850
Alabama		571	2,265	California			962
Arkansas		59	608	Connecticut....	2,801	7,844	7,693
Delaware........	3,899	12,958	18,073	Illinois		457	5,436
Florida			932	Indiana........		1,230	11,262
Georgia	398		2,931	Iowa			333
Kentucky......	114	2,759	10,011	Maine	538	929	1,356
Louisiana		10,476	17,462	Massachusetts ..	5,463	6,740	9,064
Maryland	8,043	39,730	74,723	Michigan		174	2,583
Mississippi		458	930	New Hampshire	630	786	520
Missouri		347	2,618	New Jersey	2,762	12,460	23,810
North Carolina .	4,975	14,612	27,463	New York......	4,654	29,279	49,069
South Carolina.	1,801	6,826	8,960	Ohio...........		4,723	25,279
Tennessee	361	2,727	6,422	Pennsylvania ..	6,537	30,202	53,626
Texas...........			397	Rhode Island...	3,469	3,554	3,670
Virginia	12,766	36,889	54,333	Vermont	255	903	718
....				Wisconsin			635
Total	32,357.	128,412	228,128	Total	27,109	99,281	196,016

to be enumerated as so many inhabitants, or as so much property, estimated at so much per head; or, taking a middle course, to consider them three-fifths intelligent man, and two-fifths unintelligent property; thus realizing what was *anciently* but a fabulous monster, the *Centaur*, having the head of a man and the body of a *horse*. These three plans are all adopted in the *Census Compendium*. The number of slaves in the present slaveholding States was as follows:

In 1790	. . . . .	657,527
" 1800	. . . . .	853,851
" 1810	. . . . .	1,158,459
" 1820	. . . . .	1,512,553
" 1830	. . . . .	2,001,610
" 1840	. . . . .	2,481,632
" 1850	. . . . .	3,200,304

From this it will be seen that there has been a constant increase, until there were, in 1850, over three millions; being almost one-third of the entire population of the Slave States,— more than double the population of either Norway or Denmark, — greater than that of Netherlands, Switzerland, Scotland, or Sweden, — and not quite three hundred thousand less than that of Portugal.

Some very interesting facts may be gathered from the census tables with regard to this class. If we examine, for instance, the table with regard to the "Increase and Decrease per cent. of the Slave Population of the several States at each census" (see *Appendix*), we shall see, what is indeed remarked in the *Census Compendium*, that "the increase of slaves in the southern Atlantic States has only averaged about two per cent per annum in fifty years, though averaging eighteen per cent per annum in the Gulf States, etc., for the last twenty years." Thus, in South Carolina this increase diminished from thirty-six per cent in 1790 to seventeen per cent in 1850; and, indeed, in 1840 it was but three per cent. In North Carolina it is about the same. In Maryland, from an increase it has become a decrease, and that, too, at a rapid rate. In Virginia the ratio of increase has diminished from seventeen to five per cent, and generally the ratio of increase has been of late less than that of the white population. In the Gulf States, on the other hand, the increase has in many instances been immense, and much *more rapid* than that of the white population. The cause of this is given by those who have the best opportunity to know the facts, as follows:

Hon. Henry Clay of Kentucky, in a speech, in 1829, before the Colonization Society, says: "It is believed that nowhere in the farming portion of the United States would slave labor be generally employed, if the proprietors were not tempted to raise slaves by the high price of the southern markets, which keeps it up in his own."

Professor Dew, once President of William and Mary College in Virginia, in his review of the debates in the Virginia Legislature in 1831-2, says: "From all the information we can obtain, we have no hesitation in saying that upwards of six thousand [slaves] are yearly exported [from Virginia] to other States." Again: "A full equivalent being thus left in the place of the slave, this emigration becomes an advantage to the State, and does not check the black population as much as, at first view, we might imagine; because it furnishes every inducement to the master to attend to the negroes, to encourage breeding, and to cause the greatest number possible to be raised. * * Virginia is, in fact, a negro-raising State for other States." •

The extent of this domestic slave trade is not given in De Bow's census tables, but we may, by an easy computation from the tables, arrive at something near the truth, so far as they are reliable in such matters.

On page 87 of the *Compendium*, we find the decennial increase of Slaves in the United States to be as follows: between 1790 and 1800, 27.9; between 1800 and 1810, 33.4; between 1810 and 1820, 29.1; between 1820 and 1830, 30.6; between 1830 and 1840, 23.8. The average of these ratios is 28.96. In 1840, the slave-exporting States, Delaware, Maryland, Virginia, North and South Carolina, Kentucky, and Tennessee, contained 1,479,601 slaves. Had they increased in the ratio of 28.96 per cent., the number in 1850 would have been 1,908,093. The actual number given is 1,689,158, being a difference of 218,935, or 21,893 for each year, to be accounted for. Applying the same rule to the slave-importing states, we have the following result: Georgia, Florida, Alabama, Louisiana, Mississippi, Arkansas, and Missouri contained in 1840 1,002,031 slaves. Increasing in the ratio of 28.96 per cent, their number in 1850 would have been 1,292,219. The number given in the census is 1,453,035; a difference *the other way* of 160,816, or 16,081 per year, which they had received by importation.

The difference of nearly 6,000 between the import and export may be accounted for by the following: A writer in the *New Orleans Argus*, in 1830, says: "The loss by death in bringing slaves from a northern climate, which our planters are under the necessity of doing, is not less than twenty-five per cent." And the planters in those States, when advertising for sale a plantation and a lot of negroes, always mention distinctly the fact that they are "acclimated" (if that be the case), as enhancing their value.

The number which the figures would seem to indicate as sold from the North to the South is no doubt very low; it certainly is so, if we take the estimate of Southern men. The *Virginia Times*, in 1836, estimates the number of slaves exported for sale during a single year at forty thousand.

In 1837, a committee was appointed, by the citizens of Mobile, to investigate the causes of the existing pecuniary pressure. In their report they say: "So large has been the return of slave labor, that purchases by Alabama of that species of property from other States, since 1833, have amounted to ten millions of dollars annually."

Rev. Dr. Graham, of Fayetteville, North Carolina, said in 1837: "There were nearly seven thousand slaves offered in New Orleans market last winter. From Virginia alone, six thousand were annually sent to the South; and from Virginia and North Carolina there had gone to the South, in the last twenty years, three hundred thousand slaves."

Mr. Gholson, of Virginia, in a speech in the Legislature of that State, January 18, 1831, says: "It has always (perhaps erroneously) been considered, by steady and old-fashioned people, that the owner of land had a reasonable right to its annual profits; the owner of orchards to their annual fruits; the owners of brood mares to their product; and the owners of female slaves to their increase. We have not the finespun intelligence nor legal acumen to discover the technical distinctions drawn by some gentlemen. The legal maxim of *partus sequitur ventrem* is coeval with the existence of the right of property itself, and is founded in wisdom and justice. It is on the justice and inviolability of this maxim that the master forgoes the service of the female slave, has her nursed and attended during the period of her gestation, and raises the helpless infant offspring. The value of the property justifies the expense, and I do not hesitate to say that in its increase consists much of our wealth."

The following, copied from a recent number of the *Richmond Dispatch*, will show the present condition of the trade:

"HIGH PRICE FOR SLAVES. — There has been a greater demand for slaves in this city, during the months of May, June and July, than ever known before, and they have commanded better prices during that time. The latter is an unusual thing, as the summer months are generally the dullest in the year for that description of property. Prime field hands (women) will now bring from $1,000 to $1,100, and men from $1,250 to $1,500. Not long since, a likely negro girl sold in this city, at private sale, for $1,700. A large number of negroes are bought on speculation, and probably there is not less than $1,000,000 in town, now, seeking investure in such property."

From the above, and similar sources of information, we may safely estimate the number of slaves annually sold from the Northern Slave States to the Southern at 25,000. An interesting feature of this traffic will appear on examination of the *Census Table*, showing the "ratio of ages of the slaves in 1850." *

In the States of Maryland, Virginia, North Carolina, and South Carolina, the average number of slaves between twenty and thirty years of age is 16.72 per cent. In the States of Georgia, Alabama, Mississippi, and Florida, Arkansas, Louisiana, and Texas, the number between the same ages is 19.29 per cent. In like manner, in the four first-mentioned States the average number between thirty and forty years of age is 10.27 per cent, and in the seven last mentioned it is 11.94 per cent.

* See *Census Compend.*, pp. 89–90.

On the other hand, the number between sixty and seventy years of age is, in the four exporting States, 2.76 per cent, and in the seven importing States, 1.94 per cent; also, between seventy and eighty years old, the number is, in the first four 1.16, and in the others but .55 per cent. Shówing that in the slave-importing States the number of slaves between twenty and forty years of age is at least fifteen per cent greater than in the exporting; while, on the other hand, in the slave-exporting States, the number of slaves between sixty and eighty years of age is more than fifty per cent greater than in the importing. This is the more remarkable, since *exactly the reverse* is true of the free colored population in those same States, as will be seen by a similar analysis of the table on page 75 of the *Compendium.*

Another fact with regard to the slave population of the South, and one which must soon become of great interest, is the increasing ratio of the slave to the free population. By a table on the 85th page of the *Compendium* * it will be seen that, in the words of the *Census Report,* " while the proportion has been increasing for the slaves in the Southern States generally, it has decreased in Virginia, Maryland, the District of Columbia, and Missouri." Indeed, it has increased in *most,* until it has become in Arkansas (omitting fractions), 22 per cent; in Alabama and Florida 44 per cent; in Louisiana 47 per cent; in Mississippi 51 per cent; and in South Carolina 57 per cent of the whole population; whereas it was, in 1800, in Mississippi but 39 per cent, and in South Carolina but 42 per cent; and a similar increase of the ratio of the slave to the entire population will be found in all the Southern Slave States.

* See Appendix,

CHAPTER III.

POPULAR REPRESENTATION.

THE following tables present the subject of Popular Representation in a very plain and simple manner, showing the white population, free colored, and total free population, and the popular vote cast in 1852. They also show the number of representatives in Congress, and the electoral votes, both as they now are and as they would be were freemen only represented.

TABLE VII.

Political View of the Slave States.

SLAVE STATES.	White Population.	Free Colored Population.	Total Free Population.	Popular Vote cast in 1852.	Representatives in Congress.	Representatives were not Slaves represented.	Electoral Vote as it now is.	Electoral vote were not Slaves represented.
Alabama	426,514	2,265	428,779	41,919	7	5	9	7
Arkansas	162,189	608	162,797	19,577	2	2	4	4
Delaware	71,169	18,073	89,242	12,673	1	1	3	3
Florida	47,203	932	48,135	7,193	1	1	3	3
Georgia	521,572	2,931	524,503	51,365	8	6	10	8
Kentucky	761,413	10,011	771,424	111,139	10	9	12	11
Louisiana......	255,491	17,462	272,953	35,902	4	3	6	5
Maryland......	417,943	74,723	492,666	75,153	6	6	8	8
Mississippi	295,718	930	296,648	44,424	5	3	7	5
Missouri......	592,004	2,618	594,622	65,586	7	7	9	9
North Carolina.	553,028	27,463	580,491	78,861	8	7	10	9
South Carolina.	274,563	8,960	283,523		6	3	8	5
Tennessee	756,836	6,422	763,258	115,916	10	9	12	11
Texas	154,034	397	154,431	18,547	2	2	4	4
Virginia	894,800	54,333	949,133	129,545	13	11	15	13
Total	6,184,477	228,128	6,412,605	807,800	90	75	120	105

TABLE VIII.

Political View of the Free States.

FREE STATES.	White Population.	Free Colored Population.	Total Free Population.	Popular Vote cast in 1852.	Representation in Congress.	Representation were not Slaves represented.	Electoral Vote as it now is.	Electoral Vote were not Slaves represented.
California.....	91,635	962	92,597	74,736	2	2	4	4
Connecticut ..	363,099	7,693	370,792	66,768	4	4	6	6
Illinois	846,034	5,436	851,470	155,497	9	10	11	12
Indiana	977,154	11,262	988,416	183,134	11	12	13	14
Iowa	191,881	333	192,214	16,845	2	2	4	4
Maine........	581,813	1,356	583,169	82,182	6	7	8	9
Massachusetts	985,450	9,064	994,514	132,936	11	12	13	14
Michigan	395,071	2,583	397,654	82,939	4	5	6	7
N. Hampshire.	317,456	520	317,976	52,839	3	4	5	6
New Jersey ...	465,509	23,810	489,319	83,211	5	6	7	8
New York	3,048,325	49,069	3,097,394	522,294	33	36	35	38
Ohio	1,955,050	25,279	1,980,329	353,428	21	23	23	25
Pennsylvania .	2,258,160	53,626	2,311,786	386,214	25	27	27	29
Rhode Island .	143,875	3,670	147,545	17,005	2	2	4	4
Vermont	313,402	718	314,120	43,838	3	4	5	6
Wisconsin	304,756	635	305,391	64,712	3	3	5	5
Total	13,238,670	196,016	13,434,686	2,318,578	144	159	176	191

It will be recollected that the area of the Slave States is 851,448 square miles, and that of the Free States 612,597. The white population of the Slave States is 6,184,477, and of the Free States 13,238,670. The number of free inhabitants in the Slave States is 6,412,605, and in the Free States 13,434,686. The number of freemen in the Free States is, therefore, over 600,000 *more than double* the number in the Slave States.

The representation in Congress is, from the Slave States ninety members, representing the 6,000,000; and from the Free States one hundred and forty-four, representing the 13,000,000. This discrepancy between population and representation arises from the fact that, in determining the number of representatives to which each State is entitled, five slaves are reckoned equal to three freemen. The 3,200,304 slaves, therefore, in the Slave States are reckoned equal to 1,920,182⅗

3

freemen, and are represented accordingly. The slaves of the South have, therefore, a representation equal to that of the Free States of New Hampshire, Vermont, Connecticut, Iowa, and Wisconsin.

Without the representation allowed to slave property, the number of representatives from the Slave States would be seventy-five, insteated of ninety; and from the Free States one hundred and fifty-nine, instead of one hundred and forty-four; a gain of thirty in favor of the Free States, making their representation double that of the Slave States, even without the representation of Rhode Island, Wisconsin, California, and Iowa.*

By such a change, Kentucky, Louisiana, North Carolina, and Tennessee, would lose one representative each; Alabama, Georgia, Virginia, and Mississippi, two each; and South Carolina three. Illinois, Indiana, Maine, Michigan, New Hampshire, New Jersey and Vermont would each gain one; Ohio and Pennsylvania two, and New York three.

The free population of the whole fifteen Slave States is not 9,000 more than that of the three States of New York, Pennsylvania and Massachusetts. These three States have now sixty-nine representatives.

The popular vote cast at the last Presidential election, (1852) in the Slave States was 807,800; in the Free States 2,318,578 — a majority in favor of the latter of 1,510,778, and a ratio of almost three to one. The aggregate vote of the following eleven States, viz: Maryland, Virginia, North Carolina, Georgia, Alabama, Mississippi, Louisiana, Florida, Arkansas, Delaware, and Texas, was less than that of the single State of New York; the total vote of all these States being 515,159, while that of New York was 522,294; and yet,

---

* It will be seen that in the late severe contests in the House of Representatives, had freemen only been represented, the question would invariably have been decided in favor of the North.

according to the present system of representation, these States are entitled to seventy-nine electoral votes, and New York to only thirty-five.

The three States, Massachusetts, Pennsylvania, and Ohio, or even the two States of Pennsylvania and New York, cast a popular vote larger, by more than 60,000, than *all* the Slave States. The three first named States have sixty-three electoral votes; the last two have sixty-two; and the fifteen Slave States one hundred and twenty!

In the North, 93,296 freemen and 16,101 voters are required to elect a representative to Congress. In the South, only 71,251 freemen and 8,976 voters. A President elected by the Northern votes over a candidate receiving the Southern votes would have a *popular majority* of 1,510,778 votes, or about twice the number of votes ever cast by the South.

A President elected by the South, with the votes of States enough in the North to elect him, would not be chosen by the majority. Thus, suppose a candidate to receive every vote in the South (one hundred and twenty electoral votes), and the votes of Maine, New Hampshire, Massachusetts, and Rhode Island (thirty electoral votes), this would give him one hundred and fifty electoral votes to one hundred and forty-six against him; but the popular majority against him would be almost a million of votes, or more than the whole Southern vote, as will be seen by the table, the South having 807,800 voters, and the Free States mentioned, 284,962; being a total of 1,092,762 votes; while the remaining Free States, casting but one hundred and forty-six electoral votes, would have a popular vote of 2,033,616, which is a majority of 940,854. If a President were so elected, would the North and the Northwest be justified in dissolving the Union therefor?

Or, again: suppose a President elected by the vote of the South and the vote of Pennsylvania and New Jersey, the electoral vote would be one hundred and fifty-four for him and one hundred and forty-two against him; the popular vote would be 1,277,225 for him, and 1,849,153 against him — or a majority of 571,928 votes, which is about three-quarters of the whole vote of the South. Would the Northeast and Northwest probably dissolve the Union on such a result?

CHAPTER IV.

AGRICULTURE.

THE tables found in this chapter show the condition of agriculture in the United States for the year ending June, 1850, when no other date is given.

Tables IX., X., show the number of farms and plantations, acres of cultivated land, value of the same, value per acre, value of farm implements and machinery, and whole area, in acres, of the several Free and Slave States. California is necessarily omitted from the list of the Free States, because of the defective returns of the marshals for that State. This omission can only be supplied by taking the State valuation for 1852, the first made by the State authority. In that year there were assessed for taxation in California, 6,719,442 acres of land, valued at $35,879,929, or $5.34 per acre.

In Table X., there is an evident and remarkable error — either of the marshals, or of the compiler of the census returns — in regard to the value of farms in South Carolina. This table, carefully copied from the Compendium of the Census, gives for South Carolina:

Acres improved and unimproved land, . . 16,217,600
Valued at, ... $82,431,684
" per acre, ... $5.08

Now the true value of lands in South Carolina is shown by its State valuation to differ essentially from this. Thus, in 1851, there were assessed for taxation in South Carolina (*American Almanac* for 1853, p. 278) :

Acres of land, ... 17,073,412
Valued at, ... $23,952,679
" per acre, ... $1.40

TABLE IX.

Statement showing the Number of Farms and Plantations, Acres of Improved and Unimproved Land, Cash Value of Farms, Average Value per Acre, and Value of Farming Implements and Machinery, in the several Free States, with the whole Area of each, according to the Census Returns for 1850.

FREE STATES.	Number of Farms and Plantations.	Acres of Improved Land.	Acres of Unimproved Land.	Cash Value of Farms.	Average Value per Acre.	Value of Farming Implements and Machinery.	Whole Area of States in Acres.
Connecticut	22,445	1,768,178	615,701	$72,726,422	$30.50	$1,892,541	2,991,360
Illinois	76,208	5,039,545	6,997,867	96,133,290	7.99	6,405,561	35,459,200
Indiana	93,896	5,046,543	7,746,879	136,385,173	10.66	6,704,444	21,637,760
Iowa	14,805	824,682	1,911,382	16,657,567	6.09	1,172,869	32,584,960
Maine	46,760	2,039,596	2,515,797	54,861,748	12.04	2,284,557	20,330,240
Massachusetts	34,069	2,133,436	1,222,576	109,076,347	32.50	3,209,584	4,992,000
Michigan	34,089	1,929,110	2,454,780	51,872,446	11.83	2,891,371	35,995,520
New Hampshire	29,229	2,251,488	1,140,926	55,245,997	16.28	2,314,125	5,939,200
New Jersey	23,905	1,767,991	984,955	120,237,511	43.67	4,425,503	5,324,800
New York	170,621	12,408,964	6,710,120	554,546,642	29.00	22,084,926	30,080,000
Ohio	143,807	9,851,493	8,146,000	358,758,603	19.99	12,750,585	25,576,960
Pennsylvania	127,577	8,623,619	6,294,728	407,876,099	27.27	14,722,541	29,440,000
Rhode Island	5,385	356,487	197,451	17,070,802	30.82	497,201	835,840
Vermont	29,763	2,601,409	1,524,413	63,367,227	15.36	2,739,282	6,535,680
Wisconsin	20,177	1,045,499	1,931,159	28,528,563	9.54	1,641,568	34,511,360
Total	877,736	57,688,040	50,394,734	$2,143,344,437	$19.83	$85,736,658	292,234,880

TABLE X.

Statement showing the Number of Farms and Plantations, Acres of Improved and Unimproved Land, Cash Value of Farms, Average Value per Acre, and Value of Farming Implements and Machinery, in the several Slave States, with the whole Area of each, according to the Census Returns for 1850.

SLAVE STATES.	Number of Farms and Planta-tions.	Acres of Improved Land.	Acres of Unimproved Land.	Cash Value of Farms.	Average Value per Acre.	Value of Farming Im-plements and Machinery.	Whole Area of States in Acres.
Alabama	41,964	4,435,614	7,702,067	$64,323,224	$5.30	$5,125,663	32,462,080
Arkansas	17,758	781,530	1,816,684	15,265,245	5.87	1,601,296	33,406,720
Delaware	6,063	580,862	375,282	18,880,031	19.75	510,279	1,356,800
Florida	4,304	349,049	1,246,240	6,323,109	3.97	658,795	37,931,520
Georgia	51,759	6,378,479	16,442,900	95,753,445	4.19	5,894,150	37,120,000
Kentucky	74,777	5,968,270	10,981,478	155,021,262	9.03	11,576,938	24,115,200
Louisiana	13,422	1,590,025	3,399,018	75,814,398	13.71	2,284,557	26,403,200
Maryland	21,860	2,797,905	1,836,445	87,178,545	18.81	2,463,443	7,119,360
Mississippi	33,960	3,444,358	7,046,061	54,738,634	5.22	5,762,927	30,179,840
Missouri	54,458	2,938,425	6,794,245	63,225,543	6.49	3,981,525	43,123,200
North Carolina	56,963	5,453,975	15,543,008	67,891,766	3.24	3,931,532	32,450,560
South Carolina	29,967	4,072,551	12,145,049	82,431,684	5.08	4,136,354	18,806,490
Tennessee	72,735	5,175,173	13,808,849	97,851,212	5.16	5,360,210	29,184,000
Texas	12,198	643,976	10,852,363	16,550,008	1.44	2,151,704	152,002,560
Virginia	77,013	10,360,135	15,792,176	216,401,543	8.27	7,021,772	39,265,280
Total	564,203	54,970,427	125,781,865	$1,117,649,649	$6.18	$65,345,625	544,926,720

In 1854 (*American Almanac* for 1856, p. 293), there were assessed for taxation:

Acres of land,	17,289,359
Valued at	$22,836,374
" per acre,	$1.32

As to general results, the error in the South Carolina return and the omission of California will about balance each other. By Table IX. it will be seen that the whole area in acres of the Free States, not including

California, is	292,231,880
Number of acres under cultivation,	108,082,774
" of acres not under cultivation,	184,149,106
Value of the lands under cultivation,	$2,143,344,437
" per acre,	$19.83

Whole area of the Slave States (including South Carolina, according to the incorrect

census figures)	544,742,926
Number of acres under cultivation,	180,572,292
" of acres not under cultivation,	364,170,634
Value of the land under cultivation,	$1,117,649,649
" per acre,	$6.18

Including only the lands under cultivation in the two sections, the value per acre in the North is more than three times that of the South. Including the whole area, the proportion is still larger.

The value per acre of land in the States, on the dividing line between freedom and slavery, is suggestive — thus, in the Free States, the value of farms per acre is as follows, viz:

New Jersey,	$43 67
Pennsylvania,	27 27
Ohio,	19 99
Indiana,	10 66
Illinois,	7 99
Average,	$22 17

In the border Slave States the value is as follows, viz:

Delaware,	. . . . . .	$19 75
Maryland,	. . . ، . .	18 81
Virginia, .	. . . . . .	8 27
Kentucky,	. . . . . .	9 03
Missouri,	. ،	6 49
Average,	. . . . . .	$9 25

Take those Slave States which, by position, population, or intercourse, feel least the influence of the Free States. Thus, the value of farms per acre is, in

North Carolina,	. . . . .	$3 24
South Carolina,	. . . . .	1 32
Tennessee,	. . . . . .	5 16
Florida, .	. . . . . .	3 97
Georgia, .	. . . . . .	4 19
Alabama,	. . . . . .	5 30
Arkansas,	. . . . . .	5 87
Texas, .	. . . . . .	1 44
Mississippi,	. . . . . .	5 22
Average,	. . . . . .	$3 74

Table XI. shows the value of the agricultural productions of the several Free States and Slave States for the year 1840. It is taken from the Annual Report of the Secretary of the Treasury on the Finances for 1854–5. It is understood that the articles of wheat (54,770,311 bushels in the Free States and 30,052,961 bushels in the Slave States), sugar (31,010,234 pounds in the Free States and 124,090,566 pounds in the Slave States), and molasses, are not included.

Table XII. has been prepared with great labor. In the first two columns are given the amount and value of live stock, and the amount of agricultural products, in the Free and Slave

TABLE XI.

Statement of the Value of the Agricultural Productions of the Free and of the Slave States for the year 1840.

FREE STATES.		SLAVE STATES.	
Connecticut	$11,201,618	Alabama.............	$23,833,470
Illinois	11,577,281	Arkansas	4,973,655
Indiana	14,484,610	Delaware	2,877,350
Maine	14,725,615	Georgia.....˙.......	29,612,436
Massachusetts	14,371,732	Kentucky	26,233,968
Michigan	3,207,048	Louisiana	17,976,017
New Hampshire	10,762,019	Maryland	14,015,665
New Jersey	15,314,006	Mississippi	26,297,666
New York	91,244,178	Missouri	9,755,615
Ohio	27,212,004	North Carolina	24,727,297
Pennsylvania........	51,232,204	South Carolina	20,555,919
Rhode Island........	1,951,141	Tennessee...........	27,917,692
Vermont............	16,977,664	Virginia	48,644,905
Iowa	688,308	Florida	1,817,718
Wisconsin	445,559	....	
Total..............$285,394,987		Total..............:$279,239,373	

States, for the years 1840 and 1850. In the third and fourth columns are given the values according to the calculations of De Bow, in which the products of the North and the South are calculated at the same prices, which calculation is unfavorable to the North.

As to those products whose value is given by De Bow (*Census Compendium*, p. 176), in the aggregate, their value has been distributed as follows, viz :

Eggs and feathers, according to the relative amount of poultry in the North and South in 1840.

Milk, according to amount of butter and cheese in each section in 1850.

Annual increase of stock and cattle, sheep and pigs, under one year old, according to value of live stock in 1850.

Residuum of crops, manure, etc., according to population.

Small crops, as carrots, etc., one-fourth to the South and three-fourths to the North.

In the fifth and sixth columns are given the values according
to the prices in Andrews' voluminous Report on Trade and
Commerce, made·August 19, 1852. The prices are the same
for the two sections. The aggregate products have been distributed according to the best authorities and information which
could be obtained.

In the seventh and eighth columns are given the average
crops per acre in the two sections ·as returned by the marshals
in 1850.

"The quantity of wheat in 1850," says De Bow, "is believed to be under-stated, and the crop was also short.'
"Investigations undertaken by the State legislatures and agricultural societies," says Andrews *(Report,* p. 696), "prove that
the aggregate production of wheat reported in the census tables
was below the average crop by at least 30,000,000 bushels."
It seems fair to add to our table for "understatement" the
amount of 15,000,000 bushels,* which distributed according
to production would give Free States, 10,823,899 bushels;
value $10,823,899; Slave States, 4,176,101 bushels; value,
$4,176,101.

Of hemp and flax, De Bow says: "It is impossible to
reconcile the hemp and flax returns of 1840 and 1850. No
doubt in both cases, tons and pounds have often been confounded. In a few of the States, such as Indiana and Illinois,
the returns of 1850 were rejected altogether for insufficiency."

---

* The following are the census returns of wheat, in five large wheat-
growing counties in Ohio, for 1850, and the returns made by the State
authorities for the same year:

Counties.		Census Returns.	State Returns.
Stark,	bushels,	590,594	1,071,177
Wayne,	"	571,377	1,020,000
Muskingum,	"	415,847	1,003,000
Licking,	"	336,317	849,116
Coshocton	"	416,918	852,809
		2,331,053	4,806,193

TABLE XII.

Amount of Live Stock (and its Value in 1850) and Agricultural Productions of the Free and Slave States, with the Value of the same (for 1850), according to De Bow and Andrews, for the years 1840 and 1850; and also the Average Crops, per Acre, of certain Products, according to De Bow.

Amount of Live Stock and Agricultural Productions in the United States, for the years 1840 and 1850.		Free States.	Slave States.	Value according to De Bow's prices. Free States. 1850.	Value according to De Bow's prices. Slave States. 1850.	Value according to prices in Andrews' Report. Free States. 1850.	Value according to prices in Andrews' Report. Slave States. 1850.	Average Crops per Acre. Free States.	Ave'ge Crops per Acre. Slave States.
Horses	1850	2,310,984	201,551						
Asses and Mules	1850	45,840	519,923						
Horses, Asses, and Mules	1840	2,097,305	2,236,219						
Working Oxen	1850	881,607	821,916						
Milch Cows	1850	3,626,285	2,882,525						
Other Neat Cattle	1850	4,237,928	6,079,309						
Total Neat Cattle	1840	7,597,220	7,401,062						
Sheep	1850	14,691,999	6,635,076						
"	1840	14,144,478	5,166,190						
Swine	1850	9,995,978	20,807,403						
"	1840	10,085,150	16,211,470						
Value of Live Stock	1850	$286,374,541	$253,723,687						
Value of Animals Slaughtered	1850	$56,990,247	$54,386,377	$56,990,247	$54,386,377				
Wheat, bushels	1850	72,319,491	27,903,426	72,319,491		$72,819,491	$27,903,426	12.35	9.35
"	1840	54,770,811	30,052,961						
Rye, "	1850	12,580,732	1,608,240	6,919,403	884,552	11,196,851	1,431,384	15.55	10.50
"	1840	14,321,158	4,324,409						
Oats, "	1850	96,699,002	49,882,973	29,009,701	14,904,592	42,547,561	21,948,508	26.20	16.63
"	1840	80,056,173	43,015,168						
Barley, "	1850	7,966,110	161,907	5,576,277	113,335	4,779,666	97,144	23.70	
"	1840	4,002,463	159,041						
Indian Corn, bushels	1850	242,735,176	348,992,271	121,367,588	174,496,135	145,641,106	209,395,363	31.14	18.93
"	1840	125,157,562	252,374,317						
Irish Potatoes, "	1850	59,320,970	7,705,362	23,728,388	8,082,145	39,490,727	5,779,021	118.53	112.50
Sweet "	1850	1,122,330	37,145,558	561,165	18,572,779	897,864	29,716,446		164.
Irish and Sweet Potatoes, bushels	1840	89,043,092	19,254,968						
Buckwheat, bushels	1850	8,550,618	405,347	6,669,482	316,171	4,275,309	202,673	19.62	8.50
"	1840	6,806,600	385,143						
Hay, tons	1850	12,693,661	1,187,784	88,855,627	7,964,448	158,660,762	14,222,290	1.21	1.19
"	1840	9,403,328	844,780						
Hops, pounds	1850	3,463,191	33,780	1,212,117	11,823	588,742	5,748		
"	1840	1,212,418	19,084						
Clover Seed, bushels	1850	411,152	57,820	2,055,760	289,100	2,055,760	289,100		
Other Grass Seed, bushels	1850	351,221	65,588	702,442	181,176	1,756,105	327,940		

Item	Year							Ratio
Butter, pounds	1850	245,799,578	67,249,744	$39,327,933	$10,759,959	$49,159,916	$18,449,949	11.75
Cheese, "	1850	104,077,577	1,384,490	5,203,879	69,225	6,244,655	$2,269	
Value of Dairy Products	1840	$27,494,806	$6,292,202					20.
Peas and Beans, bushels	1850	1,650,325	7,637,081	968,953	4,773,144	1,240,260	6,109,624	
Produce of Market Gardens	1850	$3,780,832	$1,377,200	3,780,332	1,377,260	36,000,000	12,000,000	
Value of Orchard Products	1850	$1,774,123	$827,073	6,347,757	1,365,927	6,347,757	1,365,927	
" " "	1840	$3,347,757	$1,365,927	1,002,242	1,274,365	1,377,802	1,592,956	
Beeswax and Honey, pounds	1850	$4,833,685	$2,420,219	5,969,411	7,030,589	9,000,000	6,000,000	
Value of Poultry, (estimated)	1850	6,889,010	7,964,780	12,767,597	7,232,403	13,500,000	6,500,000	
Cords of Wood	1840	$4,287,883	$5,053,435					
Flaxseed, bushels	1840	3,247,814	1,889,790	558,384	305,076	466,600	284,399	8.75
Flax, pounds	1850	358,923	203,384	294,328	476,021	176,897	285,612	
Hemp, tons	1850	2,948,278	4,730,208	29,793	5,217,246	26,988	4,715,528	
Hemp and Flax, tons	1840	198	34,673					
Maple Sugar, pounds	1850	26,816	68,485	1,608,240	104,284	1,608,240	104,284	
Cane Sugar, pounds	1850	32,164,799	2,085,687		12,378,850	none.	9,485,320	1.02
Cane and Maple Sugar, pounds	1840	none.	237,183,000					
Molasses, gallons	1850	31,010,234	124,090,566	110,187	2,429,149	137,732	3,086,436	
" "	1840	550,928	12,145,745	565	98,603,155	560	97,881,160	
Cotton, bales of 400 pounds	1850	14	2,445,779		4,000,000		7,320,659	16.67
" " "	1840	none.	1,976,198					
Rice, pounds	1850		215,313,497	1,082,667	12,949,398	885,143	11,099,484	
" "	1840		80,841,422					
Tobacco, pounds	1850	14,752,387	184,991,406	11,895,554	3,887,966	19,825,923	6,396,609	6.82
" "	1840	9,202,043	209,966,267					
Wool, pounds	1850	39,651,846	12,793,219					7.30
" "	1840	27,559,135	8,242,980					
Silk Cocoons, pounds	1850	5,468	5,875	2,734	2,687	2,734	2,687	
Wine, gallons	1850	174,629	44,252	349,358	88,504	87,814	22,126	
Eggs				2,453,422	2,704,073	Included with milk.		
Feathers				918,371	1,081,629	1,200,000	800,000	
Milk				5,630,745	1,369,255	11,500,000	3,500,000	
Annual Increase of Live Stock				92,750,598	82,249,402	71,593,685	63,430,922	
Cattle, Sheep and Pigs under 1 year old				26,500,171	23,499,829	75,000,000	25,000,000	
Residuum of Crops not consumed by Stock, Corn-Fodder, Straw, Seed, Cotton, Manure, &c.				58,725,718	41,274,282	Included in market gardens.		
Value of Small Crops, as Carrots, Onions, &c., Orchard and Garden Products, of Cities—Milk, Butter, Cows, Horses, &c., in Cities and Towns				15,000,000	5,000,000			
Total				$709,177,527	$634,570,057	$846,585,297	$627,101,316	

4

* In this Table the product Cotton is found in quantity nearly two and a half millions of bales, worth almost a hundred millions of dollars. Let the word Cotton never be mentioned as an article of value, without saying, that it is owing to the invention of a Northern man, stolen by law and without it, by Southern planters, that it is found in any large quantities among the agricultural products of the United States. For the treatment of Whitney, see a subsequent page.

Add, then, for "insufficiency" of returns, to the amount of hemp and flax for these two States enough to make their production in 1850 equal it in 1840, and its value will be, at six cents per pound, $1,225,138. With these corrections, the grand aggregate of the agricultural products of the United States, for the year ending June, 1850, will be, using Andrews' prices, —

Free States, ...	$858,634,334
Slave States, ...	631,277,417
Total, ...	$1,489,911,751

The following is a list of the prices of leading products in the foregoing table, by De Bow, and Andrews:

		De Bow	Andrews
Indian corn,	bushel, . .	$ 50	$ 60
Wheat,	" . .	1 00	1 00
Oats,	" . .	30	44
Irish potatoes,	" . .	40	· 75
Sweet "	" . .	50	80
Rye, "	" . .	55	89
Peas and beans,	" . .	62½	80
Cotton, bale of 400 pounds, .		40 32	40 00
Cane sugar, hhds. of 1000 lbs.		52 20	40 00
Maple sugar, pound,	. .	5	5
Butter,	" . .	16	20
Rice,	" . .	2	3 4-10
Hay, ton,	. .	7 00	12 50
Hemp, "	. .	150 47	136 00
Wool, pound,	. .	30	50
Tobacco, "	. .	7	6
Flax, "	. .	10	6

A glance at the prices of De Bow will satisfy any one that, if they be fair for Virginia, Tennessee, and the South generally, and for Illinois, Missouri, and the West, they cannot be for New England, New York, New Jersey, and Pennsylvania.

Thus of Indian corn, which De Bow calls 50 cents per bushel. If Southern and Western corn be worth that price where it is raised, Northern and Eastern corn must be worth at least 75 cents. So of wheat, which De Bow puts at a dollar. If that be fair for Tennessee, Missouri, and Illinois, a dollar and twenty-five cents is a moderate price for the Northern and Eastern States mentioned. So of oats, rye, potatoes, hay, wool, peas and beans, and some other products. There should be added then to De Bow's aggregates, for the products of New England, New York, New Jersey, and Pennsylvania, as follows, viz:

Indian corn,	56,639,174 bush. at 25 cts.	$14,159,793
Wheat,	31,183,273	"	25	7,795,818
Oats,	59,570,301	"	15	8,935,545
Rye,	11,779,509	"	20	2,355,902
Potatoes,	44,204,441	"	35	15,471,554
Hay,	9,471,369 tons,	$7	00	66,299,573
Wool,	22,283,776 lbs.		10	2,228,377
Peas and beans,	1,261,732 bush.		50	630,866

Total, ... $117,877,428

This list might be extended still further. Adding this amount to the aggregates, according to De Bow's figures, and the total amount will be, —

Free States, ...	$827,054,955
Slave States, ...	634,570,057

Total, ... $1,461,625,012

This is not essentially different from the result arrived at by taking Andrews' prices. By neither mode of calculation is full justice done to the North.

VALUE OF AGRICULTURAL PRODUCTIONS, PER ACRE, IN 1850.

The value of agricultural productions per acre for 1850 is

obtained by dividing the total product by the number of acres of land under cultivation.   Thus,—

FREE STATES.

Number of acres in farms, ...	108,193,522
Agricultural product, ...	$858,634,334
Product per acre, ...	$7,94

SLAVE STATES.

Number of acres in farms and plantations, .	180,572,392
Agricultural product, ...	$631,277,417
Product per acre, ...	$3.49

VALUE OF AGRICULTURAL PRODUCTS, PER HEAD, IN 1850.

No enumeration was made in 1850 of the whole number of persons engaged in agriculture, as was done in 1840, and the returns for the latter year must therefore be the basis of our calculation for 1850, as to the number, and the consequent value, of the products per head in the two sections of our country.   Assuming, then, that in the North the proportion of the whole population of those engaged in agriculture was the same in 1850 as in 1840, and that in the South the proportion of the free population thus engaged was no larger than in the North, we have the following result, viz :

FREE STATES.

Whole number engaged in agriculture in 1850,	2,509,126
Value of agricultural products, . .	$858,634,334
Value per head, . -	$342

SLAVE STATES.

Number of free population engaged in agriculture in 1850, ...	1,197,649
Number of slaves engaged in agriculture in 1850,	2,500,000
Total, ...	3,697,649
Value of agricultural products, . . .	$631,277,417
Value per head, . -	$171

De Bow says of the slave population of 1850 (Census Compendium, p. 94), there are "about 2,500,000 slaves directly employed in agriculture." This is a small estimate, and the number given above (1,197,649) of the 6,412,605 free population of the South engaged in agriculture is very small. With the little manufactures and commerce of the South, what are the people of that region engaged in? But, under protest, we adopt the above conclusions. This, then, is the grand result in the department of agriculture, the peculiar province of the South:

The North, with half as much land under cultivation, and two-thirds as many persons engaged in farming, produces two hundred and twenty-seven millions of dollars worth of agricultural products in a year more than the South; twice as much on an acre, and more than double the value per head for every person engaged in farming.

And this, while the South, paying nothing for its labor, has better land, a monopoly of cotton, rice, cane sugar, and nearly so of tobacco and hemp, and a climate granting two and sometimes three crops in a year. Nor does a comparison of the products of 1850 with those of 1840 afford any ground for hope for the South. A recurrence to Table XI. will show that, excluding wheat, sugar, and molasses from the aggregate, the production of the South for 1840 was nearly equal that of the North. Perhaps in 1830 it was greater.

Table XIII. gives the population, white and slave, number of acres of land, value of farms, value of land per acre, number of students and scholars in public and private schools, and the number of whites over twenty unable to read and write, in the counties in the several States on the dividing line between the Free and Slave States, from the Atlantic to the Mississippi. The statistics are from De Bow's Compendium of the Census of 1850. The table is an important one, and deserves a more extended consideration than can be given it in this work.

4*

TABLE XIII.

A Statement of Population, White and Slave, Number of acres of Land, Value of Land, Value of Farms, Value of Farms per acre, Number of Students and Scholars in Public and Private Schools, and the Number of Whites over 20 years of age unable to read and write, in the Counties on the dividing line between the Free and the Slave States, from the Atlantic to the Mississippi, with the like Statistics of the Remaining Counties of the respective States.

Border Counties and Remaining Counties of their several States.	White Population in 1850.	Slaves in 1850.	Acres of Improved and Unimproved Land in 1850.	Value of Improved and Unimproved Land in 1850.	Value of Farms per Acre.	Pupils in Colleges, Academies, and Private Schools.	White Scholars in Public Schools during the year.	No. of Whites over 5 and under 20 years old.	No. of Whites over 20 unable to read & write.
Counties of Delaware adjacent to New Jersey	50,849	741	501,667	$15,848,700	$31.59	2,075	10,596	18,707	6,292
The remaining County of Delaware	20,320	1,549	454,667	3,541,550	7.79	80	3,620	7,902	3,485
Counties of New Jersey adjacent to Delaware	47,486		386,720	14,553,731	37.63	185	10,642	17,628	1,120
Remaining Counties of New Jersey	418,023		2,366,226	105,683,781	44.66	10,129	78,683	148,253	11,667
County of Pennsylvania adjoining Delaware	23,122		105,569	9,067,082	85.89	303	5,142	8,320	422
Counties of Maryland adjoining Pennsylvania	315,282	17,430	1,615,227	47,851,615	29.63	10,386	42,885	105,229	19,208
Remaining Counties of Maryland	102,661	72,988	3,019,123	41,790,873	13.84	1,528	17,562	42,488	19,158
Counties of Pennsylvania adjoining Maryland	330,688		2,799,592	105,186,277	37.56	3,245	77,376	123,613	11,473
Counties of Virginia adjoining Pennsylvania	64,540	527	732,913	9,512,647	12.98	867	10,505	24,368	4,001
Remaining Counties of Virginia	880,260	472,001	25,419,888	213,910,668	8.42	9,544	99,206	320,897	83,382
Counties of Pennsylvania adjoining Virginia	128,927		1,873,119	32,985,617	24.74	1,830	31,283	49,350	3,708
Remaining Counties of Pennsylvania	2,129,233		13,545,228	374,890,482	27.68	25,941	466,828	775,320	47,575
Counties of Virginia adjacent to Ohio	88,251	1,689	980,219	5,543,846	5.65	150	5,677	15,614	3,845
Counties of Ohio adjacent to Virginia	97,963		843,545	9,354,429	11.09	762	22,874	38,463	4,998
Remaining Counties of Ohio	1,853,087		17,153,948	349,404,174	20.37	17,911	489,904	719,170	51,960
Counties of Kentucky adjacent to Ohio	81,749	9,672	926,151	66,923,361	18.27	942	12,327	30,944	4,422
Counties of Ohio adjacent to Kentucky	261,724		1,069,308	34,577,488	32.34	5,994	48,102	91,906	8,334
Counties of Kentucky adjacent to Indiana	106,473	28,731	1,053,014	17,250,889	10.44	2,764	16,267	39,308	5,252
Remaining Counties of Kentucky	654,940	182,251	15,296,746	142,889,410	9.34	11,721	114,650	263,596	62,107
Counties of Indiana adjacent to Kentucky	134,509		1,276,989	14,480,233	11.34	1,114	26,665	45,657	7,075
Remaining Counties of Indiana	842,645		11,516,433	121,904,940	10.59	6,140	198,369	353,635	62,370
Counties of Kentucky adjacent to Illinois	27,443	5,908	627,218	2,918,419	4.65	388	5,235	11,085	2,700
Counties of Illinois adjacent to Kentucky	18,101		235,716	1,098,685	4.54	none.	2,307	7,384	1,861
Remaining Counties of Illinois	826,933		11,801,696	95,089,604	8.05	4,686	179,662	328,079	38,575

In proportion to the white population, these border counties of the Slave States contain the following per cent of slaves, viz :

Delaware, ... 1 per cent.
Maryland, ... 5 "
Virginia, ... 2 "
Kentucky, ... 21 "

The remaining counties of the same States give the following, viz :

Delaware, ... 8 per cent.
Maryland, ... 71 "
Virginia, ... 59 "
Kentucky, ... 31 "

The value of lands per acre will be seen by an examination of the table; and it will be noticed, that, with the exception of the broken region of Virginia, which lies adjacent to Ohio, and that of Kentucky, which lies adjacent to Illinois, the value of lands per acre in the counties of the Slave States adjoining the Free is greater than that of the remaining counties of their respective States. The opposite is true, generally, of the border counties of the Free States. Thus, the effects of freedom and slavery on the value of the adjacent lands is reciprocal. The neighborhood of slavery lessens their value in the Free States; the neighborhood of freedom increases it in the Slave States. To such an extent is this true, that, in Virginia, for example, the lands in counties naturally poor, are, by the proximity of freedom, rendered more valuable than those unequalled lands in the better portions of the State. Indeed, this table shows the fact that the lands in the border counties of the Slave States are worth more per acre than the remaining lands in the same States, with the addition of the value of the whole number of their slaves at $400 per head. And this, be it remembered, while the value of lands in the balance of the counties of the border Slave States is double that of the lands in the Slave States not adjacent to the Free. It is for the interest of the Slave States to be hedged in by a circle of Free States. If Tennessee had been a Free State, her lands would have been worth as much as those of Ohio, — $19.99 per acre, instead of $5.16 as now, — and who cannot see that, in that event, the lands of North Carolina, South Carolina, and Georgia would have been worth more per acre than the sums of $3.24, $1.40, $4.19, respectively. Not only could Tennessee afford to sacrifice the whole value of her slaves for the sake of freedom, but even North Carolina, South Carolina, and Georgia could afford to sacrifice the whole value of their own slaves, and pay for all of the slaves in Tennessee for the sake of having a free neighbor. The increased value of lands would more than compensate for the sacrifice. The figures prove this.

Tennessee has 18,984,022 acres of land under cultivation, worth $5.16 per acre. Multiply this number of acres by $14.83 (the difference between the value of lands in Tennessee and Ohio), and the amount is, . . . $281,533,046

Tennessee has 239,459 slaves; value, at $400 each, ... 95,783,600

This leaves the respectable margin of . . 185,749,446

North Carolina, South Carolina, and Georgia have 60,891,774 acres of land, worth $3 08 per acre. Multiply this number of acres by $15.73 (the difference in value between the lands in these States and the border Slave State of Maryland), and the amount is . $957,827,605

Number of slaves in these States, . . . 1,055,214

Value at $400 each, ... $422,085,600

Value of slaves in Tennessee, as above, . . 95,783,600

Total, ... $517,869,200

Deducting this from the increased value of lands, and the balance in favor of free neighbors is the sum of $439,958,405

Thus, the figures show that Tennessee could afford, for the sake of freedom, to sacrifice the whole value of her quarter of a million of slaves, and pay in addition the sum of $185,749,446. For the sake of a free neighbor, and to bring up their lands to the value of those of Maryland, the States of North and South Carolina, and Georgia, could afford to sacrifice the whole of their own slaves, pay for those of Tennessee, and make $439,958,405 by the bargain, which sum is considerably more than twice the present value of all their lands. Nay, these States could afford to send off, singly, every slave within their limits, in a coach with two horses, and provisions for a year, if they could but bring up the value of their lands to that of the land in northern Maryland. Indignation, and patriotism, and dissolution of the Union, indeed, if a fugitive now and then be not reclaimed! South Carolina could afford to pay every year more money than she spent in the whole Revolutionary war, to make her whole number of slaves fugitives; and then make money enough by the transaction to fence in the whole State with a picket fence, to prevent their return.

NEW ENGLAND, SOUTH CAROLINA, AND VIRGINIA.

Comparisons between portions of the North and the South can be made to any extent. A few are added, with such suggestions as seem proper.

Table XIV. is a comparison between the States of Rhode Island and Connecticut, and an equal extent of cultivated lands in certain counties of South Carolina. The table includes the city of Charleston. The comparison extends to the value of lands, population, value of agricultural and manufactured products, commerce, and education. The value of lands in the South Carolina counties is the fictitious one of De Bow's Compendium, and not the real one of the State valuation.

The portions compared in Table XIV. are of equal age as well as extent. The free portion has eleven times the white population; nearly four times the total population of white and slave. Its lands are worth six times as much, and twice as much after

TABLE XIV.

A Statement of the Acres of Land in Farms, Cash Value thereof, Value per acre, White and Slave Population, with the Value of the Slaves and their Value per acre, Value of Agricultural and Manufacturing Products, Amount of Tonnage owned, and built in 1855, and the number of Students in Colleges, &c., and Scholars in Public Schools, in the States of Rhode Island and Connecticut, and an equal area in South Carolina.

States.	Acres of Improved Land in 1850.	Acres of Unimproved Land in 1850.	Cash Value of Farms in 1850.	Cash Value of Farms per acre, 1850.	White Population in 1850.	Slaves in 1850.	Value of Slaves per acre, at $400 each.	Value of Slaves at $400 each.	Value of Agricultural Products in 1850, according to De Bow.	Value of Manufactures in 1850.	Tonnage owned June 30, 1855.	Tonnage built during the year ending June 30, 1855.	Students in Colleges, Academies, and Private Schools, 1850.	Scholars in Public Schools, 1850.
Connecticut ...	1,768,178	615,701	$74,618,963	$31.34	363,099				$8,686,789	$45,302,354	187,170	14,067	7,734	71,269
Rhode Island..	356,487	197,451	17,568,003	31.55	143,875				1,683,974	22,119,753	51,088	7,862	1,884	23,130
Total	2,124,665	813,151	$92,186,966	$31.37	506,974				$10,270,763	$67,422,107	188,808	21,929	9,618	94,399
Counties in South Carolina of area equal to Rhode Island & Connecticut.														
Charleston	188,236	636,495	$5,903,220	$7.20	25,208	54,775	$26.85	$21,910,000	$896,904	$2,767,760	56,419	61	3,082	1,196
Georgetown ...	49,609	318,514	5,704,920	15.49	2,193	18,253	19.83	7,301,200	1,104,685	68,619	4,516		281	170
Williamsburg .	70,380	432,440	861,588	1.71	3,902	8,508	6.11	3,403,200	223,740	12,825			none.	378
Horry	33,664	472,971	385,840	.76	5,522	2,075	1.63	830,000	160,640	154,684			"	488
Marion........	124,306	652,342	2,680,544	3.45	9,781	7,520	3.87	3,008,000	377,826	40,624			50	850
Total	461,175	2,512,762	$15,536,062	$5.19	46,606	91,131	$12.17	$36,452,400	$2,763,795	$3,044,412	60,935	61	3,413	2,582

adding to the value of the lands the whole value of the slaves in this most intensely slave portion of the Union, at the rate of $400 for each slave. The value of the agricultural products of Connecticut and Rhode Island is four times as great as that of those of this portion of Carolina, although the latter has the monopoly almost of the rice-producing region. Of the value of the Carolina products, one-third is cotton; and here is the place to say, that it is owing to the invention of a Massachusetts man that the South is able to raise its cotton at all at this time. If the South had been obliged to clean cotton by hand, at the rate of a pound a day for each slave, as before the invention of Whitney, the whole cotton-producing region would have been bankrupt. The treatment which the Northern inventor received at the hands of those Southrons, whose fortunes he had made, is a sad portion of history. Before his patent was obtained, a mob of the chivalry (who despise so heartily and magnificently a money-making, peddling Yankee) broke open the building in which his machine was placed, carried off the machine, and made others from it; and, before he could go through the formalities of getting his patent, several machines were in successful operation on the plantations of different gentlemen. In the Georgia courts, Whitney's rights were decided against, on the ground mainly that, as "the introduction of the gin would open up boundless resources of wealth to the planters, it was too great a power to allow any one man a monopoly of the right to furnish the machines." South Carolina agreed to pay $50,000 for the invention, paid $20,000 down, then repudiated the contract, sued Whitney and his partner for the money paid, and cast the latter into prison. Afterwards, this action was reversed and the contract fulfilled. The action of Tennessee was similar to that of South Carolina, without the repentance. North Carolina did better, and was faithful to its contract. After years of litigation, Whitney got a decision in his favor in the United States Court; but meantime his patent was nearly out, and his application for a renewal was denied by the votes of those whose fortunes he had made. In Georgia, in the courts,

witnesses, judges, and juries gave way, in spite of law and
evidence, before the rapacity of the planters. "In one instance," says Whitney, "I had great difficulty in proving
that the machine had been used in Georgia, although at the
same moment there were three separate sets of this machinery
in motion within fifty yards of the building in which the court
sat, and all so near that the rattling of the wheels was distinctly
heard on the steps of the court-house."

To return to table XIV. In manufactures, the North has
more than twenty times; in tonnage owned in 1855, three
times; and in tonnage built in the same year, three hundred
and fifty times as much as the South. The "tonnage built"
in 1855, in South Carolina, consisted of one schooner of sixty-
one tons burden. This is since the sitting of several Southern
conventions, in which they resolved to have an extensive commerce of their own, not only with Europe, but with Brazil and
Central America. As to education, the New England figures
are twenty times as large as those of Carolina.

Table XV. is a comparison between Massachusetts and an
equal extent of territory in Virginia. The portion of Virginia
taken is the southeastern, from the Atlantic to the mountains.
It includes Norfolk, the commercial capital of Virginia, and the
land taken is naturally as good as that of other parts of the
State, and much better than the lands in Massachusetts. The
age of the two sections is about the same. As compared with
Virginia, the white population in Massachusetts is ten times as
great, and five times as great as its total white and slave. Her
lands are worth nearly six times as much per acre, and almost
twice as much as the lands and slaves of the Virginia counties
added together, although they constitute the most dense slave
section of the State (the slaves being worth twice as much as
the lands and buildings). The agricultural products of Massachusetts, at De Bow's prices, are nearly double those of the
Virginia counties, while her manufacturing products are more
than forty times as great, and eight times as much in a single year
as the whole value of this great portion of Virginia, including

TABLE XV.

A Statement of the Number of Acres in Farms, Value of Farms, Value of the same per acre, White and Slave Population, Value of Slaves, Value of Agricultural and Manufacturing Products, Tonnage owned, and built in 1855, Pupils in Colleges, &c., and Number of Scholars in the Public Schools, in the State of Massachusetts, and an equal area in Virginia.

Counties in Virginia of area equal to the State of Massachusetts.	Acres of Improved Land in 1850.	Acres of Unimproved Land in 1850.	Cash value of Farms in 1850.	Cash Value of Farms per acre in 1850.	White Population in 1850.	Slaves in 1850.	Value of Slaves per Acre at $400 per Slave.	Value of Slaves at $400 per Slave.	Value of Agricultural Products in 1850, according to De Bow.	Value of Manufactures, 1850.	Tonnage Owned June 30, 1855.	Amount of Tonnage Built in 1855.	Pupils in Colleges, Academies, and Private Schools, 1850.	Scholars in the Public Schools in 1850.
Patrick	88,192	184,034	$734,771	$3.31	7,187	2,824	$4.18	$929,600	$246,326	$140,172			none.	826
Henry	61,539	93,409	820,070	5.19	5,324	3,340	8.45	1,336,000	258,525	99,956			"	1,391
Pittsylvania	210,580	300,295	2,850,908	5.58	15,263	12,798	10.02	5,119,200	925,141	878,660			142	667
Halifax	242,758	202,291	3,420,990	7.68	10,976	14,452	12.98	5,780,800	1,128,810	287,666			none.	283
Mecklenburg	215,646	179,183	2,585,628	5.12	7,256	12,462	10.07	4,984,800	831,248	226,654			239	574
Brunswick	177,196	117,702	1,097,948	3.68	4,985	8,456	11.46	3,382,400	524,157	44,941			86	186
Greenville	74,906	82,066	427,173	2.72	1,731	3,785	9.64	1,514,000	198,936	17,641			30	95
Sussex	91,408	98,677	600,096	3.15	3,086	5,992	12.60	2,396,800	328,892	80,133			14	235
Southampton	159,668	176,023	1,068,103	3.28	5,940	5,755	7.06	2,302,000	456,902	36,600			68	288
Nansemond	62,398	117,968	1,711,090	9.52	5,424	4,715	10.46	1,886,000	355,055	168,751			174	298
Norfolk	89,014	75,866	1,252,031	10.89	20,329	10,400	36.21	4,160,000	297,209	1,412,594	35,051	2,171	363	1,926
Princess Anne	50,064	63,175	1,110,673	8.67	4,280	3,130	11.05	1,252,000	257,835	33,337			none.	819
Isle of Wight	65,925	92,901	982,939	6.18	4,710	3,395	8.55	1,358,000	257,046	58,432			56	149
Surry	44,298	65,463	562,052	5.12	2,215	2,479	8.95	991,600	158,347	19,948			30	150
Total	1,583,502	1,852,056	$19,080,472	$5.64	98,606	93,488	$11.04	$37,393,200	$6,224,329	$3,504,885	35,051	2,171	1,202	7,892
Massachusetts	2,133,433	1,222,576	$109,076,347	$32.50	985,450				$11,003,887	$151,342,478	970,727	79,620	14,479	176,475

5

its commercial capital. Tonnage owned, Massachusetts twenty-eight parts, Virginia one part; tonnage built in 1855, Massachusetts thirty-seven parts, Virginia one part. Education, scholars, Massachusetts twenty-one parts, Virginia one part.

TABLE XVI.

Population, Crops, and other Statistics of Plymouth and Norfolk Counties, in Massachusetts, and James City and Westmoreland Counties, in Virginia, for the year 1850.

Population, Crops, &c.	Plymouth County, Mass.	James City County, Va.	Norfolk County, Mass.	Westmoreland County, Va.
Whites	55,241	1,489	78,643	3,376
Free Colored....................	456	663	249	1,147
Slaves		1,868		3,557
Total..........................	55.697	4,020	78.892	8,080
Dwellings......................	9,506	396	12.545	869
Whites between the ages of 5 and 20	17,342	540	23,460	1,330
Pupils in public & private schools	11,249	315	18,252	367
Natives unable to read and write, over 20 years of age	50	52	64	398
Number of Farms................	2,447	129	2,637	443
Acres of Improved Land........	101,135	21,251	107,884	68,627
Acres of Unimproved Land	114.254	44,132	67,444	6,450
Value of Farms.................	$6,048.442	$561,931	$13,748.505	$1,132.197
Value of Farms per acre........	$28.08	$8.59	$78.41	$8.70
Number of Horses and Mules....	2,458	534	3.311	1,101
" " Neat Cattle..........	11,855	2.365	12,656	6,225
" " Sheep..............	5,384	1,217	580	3,676
" " Swine..............	4,574	4,009	8,209	8,237
Wheat, bushels	251	25,476	356	82,774
Rye, "	17.143		17,423	502
Oats, "	26,809	22,040	14.939	7,897
Indian Corn, bushels...........	105,243	102,430	112.132	269,115
Irish Potatoes, "	208,402	2,789	253,158	4,970
Sweet Potatoes, "		5,730		6,176
Peas and Beans, "	871	300	3,952	1,350
Barley, "	3.267		5,462	
Buckwheat, "	239		454	
Butter, pounds	374.816	17,785	347,089	28,437
Cheese, "	130,478		90,160	
Hay, tons	28,532	8	41,588	32
Hops, pounds...................	12		81	129
Clover Seed, bushels.............	152			
Other Grass Seed, bushels				1,346
Tobacco, pounds................				7
Cotton, bales				
Wool, pounds...................	16,643	2,197	879	8,603
Beeswax and Honey, pounds.....	3,352		1,047	3,700
Value of Animals slaughtered....	$176,102	$14.339	$289,809	$41,740
Value of Produce of Market Gard's	$13,502	$365	$136,796	$26
" " Orchard Products.......	$19,205		$55,458	$512
Wine, gallons..................	21		91	2
Manufacturing Capital	$2,397.305	none.	$5,433,300	$3,330
Number of Hands...............	8,024	"	15,628	19
Annual Product................	$6,713.906	"	$13,323,595	$16,300
Value of Domestic Manufactures .	$953	$544	$25,702	$7,843

Table XVI. is a comparison between the counties of Norfolk and Plymouth in Massachusetts, and the counties of Westmoreland and James City in Virginia, as to population, education, agriculture, etc.

James City Co. is the county in which are situated Jamestown, the Plymouth of Virginia, and William and Mary's College, the rival in age of Harvard University. Jamestown now contains two houses, and of William and Mary's College it is said that it seldom has more than forty students (the Census Compendium gives it thirty-five in 1850). Westmoreland Co. is the native county of Washington. Of the Massachusetts counties, Norfolk is the county of the Adamses, and Plymouth that of the Pilgrim settlement.

VALUE OF LAND IN NORTHERN AND SOUTHERN COUNTIES.

The value of land per acre in some of the counties in the South, where there is the largest proportion of slaves, is as follows, viz:

Charles Co., Maryland (whites 5,665; slaves 9,584), $10.50.

Amelia Co., Virginia (whites, 2,785; slaves, 6,819), $7.60.

Beaufort, Colleton, and Georgetown Co.'s, South Carolina (whites, 14,915; slaves, 71,904), $7.30.

The value of land per acre in some Northern counties is as follows, viz: Hudson Co., New Jersey, $178; Delaware Co., Pennsylvania, $86.

No more tables will be given in the department of agriculture. Some further comparisons and illustrations are given.

Virginia, free, and as thickly settled as Massachusetts, would have had, in 1850, 7,751,324 whites instead of 894,800.

Massachusetts, a slave State, and as thinly populated as Virginia, would have had in 1850, 102,351 white inhabitants instead of 985,450.

Virginia, free, would have had an annual product of manufactures amounting to $1,190,072,592. instead of $29,705,387.

Massachusetts, a slave State, would have had manufactures amounting to $3,776,601, instead of $151,137,145.

Virginia, free, would have been worth in real and personal property (on the basis of the census estimate), $4,333,525,367, instead of (value of slaves deducted) $203,635,238.

Massachusetts, a slave State, would have been worth $48,604,335 instead of $551,106,824.

Boston, with slavery, according to the increase of population in Virginia, would have contained 3,489 people instead of 136,881. In the whole South there are less than fifty cities with a population of 3,500.

Richmond, Virginia, free, according to the increase of population in Massachusetts, would have contained 1,076,669 free people instead of 17,643.

If Virginia had not a settler within her territory, and should be opened at once to free settlement, in ten years she would have nearly as many white inhabitants as she now has, two hundred and fifty years after her settlement, and in twenty years she would have nearly as many whites as the whole number of slaveholding States now have, provided 60,000 settlers should go in the first year, and that the rate of increase should be as great as that of Wisconsin, Iowa, or Minnesota. Even with this population of twenty years, she would not be so densely peopled as Massachusetts was in 1850. The figures prove our statements: thus, Wisconsin had, in 1840, 30,749 whites; in 1850, 304,756. Ratio of increase 89.11 per cent. Assume 60,000 whites in Virginia at the close of the first year, and the rate of increase as above, then in ten years she would have 594,660 white inhabitants, and in twenty years 5,793,475. Number of whites in Virginia in 1850, 894,800; in the slaveholding States, 6,184,477. Thus, as to population, slavery in two hundred and fifty years has done the work of twenty. As to the value of lands, it has done still worse. Thus, in little more than ten years, Wisconsin had brought up the value of her farms per acre to $9.54; Virginia in two hundred and fifty years had barely raised the price of her lands to $8.27.

We give below, from different authorities, the past and present condition of the lands of the Free and Slave States.

"New England" (says "A perfect description of Virginia," published in London in 1649) "is in a good condition of livelihood; but for matter of any great hope but fishing there is not much." Compared to Virginia, "it's as Scotland is to England, so much difference, and lies upon the same land northward as Scotland does to England; there is much cold, frost, and snow; their land is barren, except a herring be put into the hole you set the corn in, it will not come up; and it was a great pity all those planters, now about 20,000, did not seat themselves at first at the south of Virginia, in a warm and rich country, where their industry could have produced sugar, indigo, ginger, cotton, and the like commodities."

Said Sir Thomas Dale, in 1612, speaking of Virginia, "Take four of the best kingdoms in Christendom, and put them all together, they may no way compare with this country either for commodities or goodness of soil."

Says Beverley at a later period: "In extreme fruitfulness, it (Virginia) is exceeded by no other. No seed is sown there but it thrives, and most of the northern plants are improved by being transplanted thither."

Says Lane, the Governor of Raleigh colony, in 1585, speaking of Virginia and Carolina: "It is the goodliest soil under the cope of heaven, the most pleasing territory of the world. The climate is so wholesome that we have not one sick since we touched the land. If Virginia had but horses and kine, and were inhabited with English, no realm in Christendom were comparable to it."

Such was the country which slavery took two hundred years ago: and any quantity of testimony to its fertility could be quoted. Mark the change which slavery has made.

Says Washington (letter to Arthur Young, Nov. 1, 1787),

" Our lands, as I mentioned to you, were originally very good, but use and abuse have made them quite otherwise."

Says Olmsted (Seaboard Slave States, pages 63 and 65), speaking of the lands, stock, and vehicles of a certain locality in eastern Virginia in 1855 : " Oldfields' — a coarse, yellow, sandy soil, bearing scarce anything but pine trees and broom-sedge. In some places, for acres, the pines would not be above five feet high — that was land that had been in cultivation, used up, and 'turned out' not more than six or eight years before; then there were patches of every age; sometimes the trees were a hundred feet high. At long intervals there were fields in which the pine was just beginning to spring in beauti-ful green plumes from the ground, and was yet hardly noticeable among the dead brown grass and sassafras bushes and black-berry vines, which nature first sends to hide the nakedness of the impoverished earth.

" Of living creatures, for miles, not one was to be seen (not even a crow or a snow-bird), except hogs. These — long, lank, snake-headed, hairy, wild beasts — would come dashing across our path, in packs of from three to a dozen, with short hasty grunts, almost always at a gallop, and looking neither to the right nor left, as if they were in pursuit of a fox, and were quite certain to catch him in the next hundred yards." (Num-ber of swine in Virginia in 1850, 1,829,843.)

" We turned the corner, following some slight traces of a road, and shortly afterwards met a curious vehicular establish-ment, probably belonging to the master of the hounds. It consisted of an axle-tree and wheels, and a pair of shafts, made of unbarked saplings, in which was harnessed, by attachments of raw-hide and rope, a single small ox. There was a bit made of telegraph wire in his mouth, by which he was guided, through the mediation of a pair of much knotted rope-reins, by a white man — a dignified sovereign wearing a brimless crown — who sat upon a two-bushel sack (of meal, I hope, for the hounds' sake), balanced upon the axle-tree; and who saluted me with a frank ' How are you ? ' as we came opposite each other."

Said Henry A. Wise, in 1855, during his canvass for Govenor, speaking to the Virginians : " You all own plenty of land, but it is poverty added to poverty. Poor land added to poor land, and nothing added to nothing makes nothing ; while the owner is talking politics at Richmond, or in Congress, or spending the summer at the White Springs, the lands grow poorer and poorer, and this soon brings land, negroes, and all, under the hammer. You have the owners skinning the negroes, and the negroes skinning the land, until all grow poor together.

" You have relied alone on the single power of agriculture, and such agriculture ! Your sedge-patches outshine the sun ; your inattention to your only source of wealth has scared the bosom of mother Earth. Instead of having to feed cattle on a thousand hills, you have to chase the stump-tailed steer through the sedge-patches to procure a tough beef-steak." (Number of neat cattle in Virginia, in 1850, 1,076,269.)

" I have heard a story — I will not locate it here or there — about the condition of the prosperity of our agriculture. I was told by a gentleman in Washington, not long ago, that he was travelling in a county not a hundred miles from this place, and overtook one of our citizens on horseback, with perhaps, a bag of hay for a saddle, without stirrups, and the leading line for a bridle, and he said, ' Stranger, whose house is that?' 'It is mine,' was the reply. They came to another. 'Whose house is that?' 'Mine, too, stranger.' To a third, 'And whose house is that?' 'That's mine, too, stranger; but don't suppose I'm so darned poor as to own all the *land* about here.'"

Wise was speaking at Alexandria, in Fairfax Co., the county of Mount Vernon, and the farm of Washington. In certain parts, this county has been wonderfully improved by Northern emigrants, who have purchased lands and applied free labor and skill to them. So much have they improved their portion, that the Patent Office Report says, "A traveller who passed over it ten years ago would not now recognize it."

Says the Hon. Willoughby Newton, of Virginia, in his agricultural address, in 1850: "I look upon the introduction of *guano*, and the success attending its application to our barren lands, in the light of a *special interposition of Divine Providence*, to save the northern neck of Virginia from reverting into its former state of wilderness and utter desolation. Until the discovery of guano — more valuable to us than the mines of California — I looked upon the possibility of renovating our soil, of ever bringing it to a point capable of producing remunerating crops, as utterly hopeless." Is Virginia to be saved by guano? Mr. Newton recommends the application of two hundred pounds per acre. Number of acres of land under cultivation in Virginia in 1850, 26,152,311. Amount of guano requisite to cover this land, at the rate of two hundred pounds per acre, 2,615,231 tons. This, at $50 per ton, would cost $130,761,550. Guano must be applied every other year. This would give the annual amount 1,307,615 tons, and the annual cost $65,380,775. Where is the money to pay this annual tax to come from? How long would it take the permanent registered tonnage of Virginia (9,246 tons in 1855) to import enough for one year's use? And then the spectacle of this magnificent fleet (of eighteen vessels of five hundred tons, or thirty of three hundred), officered by the chivalry, and manned by slaves, toting bird-manure around Cape Horn, in quantities enough to cover the worn-out surface of the Old Dominion!

Of North Carolina, the Patent Office Report for 1851 says (communication of G. S. Sullivan, of Lincoln Co.), "We raise no stock of any kind except for home consumption, and not half enough of that; for we have now worn out our lands so much, that we do not grow food enough to maintain them."

Of Alabama (communication of N. B. Powell): "We are

the most dependent people in the Union, rely mainly, as we do, upon our neighbors of the West for nearly all our supplies."

Says Olmsted (page 475) of the threshing of rice in South Carolina: "Threshing commences immediately after harvest, and on many plantations proceeds very tediously, in the old way of threshing wheat with flails by hand, occupying the best of the plantation force for the most of the winter. It is done on an earthen floor in the open air, and the rice is cleaned by carrying it on the heads of the negroes, by a ladder, up on to a platform, twenty feet from the ground, and pouring it slowly down, so that the wind will drive off the chaff, and leave the grain in a heap under the platform." Threshing machines have, however, been introduced on some large plantations.

Of Alabama, says Hon. C. C. Clay, Jr., a politician and leading man, in an address in 1855: "I can show you, with sorrow, in the older portions of Alabama, and in my native county of Madison, the sad memorials of the artless and exhausting culture of cotton. Our small planters, after taking the cream off their lands, unable to restore them by rest, manures, or otherwise, are going farther west and south, in search of other virgin lands, which they may and will despoil and impoverish in like manner."

"In 1825, Madison county cast about 3,000 votes; now she cannot cast exceeding 2,300. In traversing that county, one will discover numerous farm-houses, once the abode of industrious and intelligent freemen, now occupied by slaves, or tenantless, deserted, and dilapidated; he will observe fields, once fertile, now unfenced, abandoned, and covered with those evil harbingers — fox-tail and broom-sedge; he will see the moss growing on the mouldering walls of once thrifty villages; and will find 'one only master grasps the whole domain' that once furnished happy homes for a dozen white families. Indeed, a county in its infancy, where fifty years ago scarce a forest tree had been felled by the axe of the pioneer, is already exhibiting the painful signs of senility and decay, apparent in

Virginia and the Carolinas; the freshness of its agricultural glory is gone; the vigor of its youth is extinct, and the spirit of desolation seems brooding over it."

Enough of these extracts to show the blight of slavery in the department of agriculture; no extracts are needed to show that the farms in the Free States increase in value with every succeeding year. It is not now necessary "that a herring be put into the hole" with corn, "or it will not come up."

CHAPTER V.

MANUFACTURES.

THE tables in this chapter, compiled — when no other authority is given — from the Compendium of the Census of 1850, show the state of manufactures in the United States for the year ending June, 1850. The tables for 1850 are preceded by tables (from the annual Report of the Secretary of the Treasury on the Finances, for 1855) giving the population, and value of the manufactures, of the several Free and Slave States for the years 1820 and 1840. The returns for 1820 were defective in some particulars, and the article of sugar is included among the manufactures for 1840.

TABLE XVII.

Population and Value of Manufactures in the Free States, for the years 1820 and 1840.

FREE STATES.	Population in 1820.	Population in 1840.	Value of Manufactures for 1820.	Value of Manufactures for 1840.
Connecticut	275,202	309,978	$2,413,029	$21,057,523
Illinois	55,211	476,183	100,983	8,021,582
Indiana	147,178	685,866	397,814	9,379,586
Iowa		43,112		483,700
Maine............	298,335	501,793	486,473	14,525,217
Massachusetts	523,287	737,699	2,523,614	73,777,837
Michigan.........	8,896	212,267	100,460	3,898,676
New Hampshire...	244,161	284,574	747,959	10,523,313
New Jersey.......	277,575	373,306	1,175,139	19,571,496
New York........	1,372,812	2,428,921	9,792,072	95,840,194
Ohio	581,434	1,519,467	5,290,427	31,458,401
Pennsylvania	1,049,458	1,724,033	6,895,219	64,494,960
Rhode Island.....	83,059	108,830	1,617,221	13,807,297
Vermont	235,764	291,948	890,353	6,923,982
Wisconsin........		30,945		1,680,808
Total	5,152,372	9,698,922	$32,430,763	$375,444,572

TABLE XVIII.

Population and Value of Manufactures in the Slave States, for the years 1820 and 1840.

SLAVE STATES.	Population in 1820.	Population in 1840.	Value of Manufactures for 1820.	Value of Manufactures for 1840.
Alabama.........	127,901	590,756	$101,207	$4,975,871
Arkansas	14,273	97,574	56,408	2,614,882
Delaware	72,749	78,085	1,318,891	2,709,068
Florida		54,477		915,080
Georgia	340,987	691,392	607,751	5,324,307
Kentucky	564,317	779,828	2,296,726	13,221,958
Louisiana	153,407	352,411	272,500	11,378,383
Maryland	407,350	470,019	5,027,336	13,509,636
Mississippi	75,448	375,651	none.	3,562,370
Missouri	66,586	383,702	297,443	5,946,759
North Carolina ...	638,829	753,419	445,398	7,234,567
South Carolina ...	502,741	594,398	168,666	5,638,823
Tennessee........	422,813	829,210	2,352,127	8,517,394
Virginia..........	1,065,379	1,239,797	6,686,699	20,684,608
Total	4,452,780	7,290,719	$19,631,152	$106,233,713

Taking tables XX. and XIX. without the modifications suggested hereafter, and the relation of the North and South to manufactures in 1850, was as follows, viz:

	In the North.	In the South.
Capital invested in manufactures.....$	430,240,051	$ 95,029,879
Value of raw material used.........	465,844,092	86,190,639
Number of hands employed, males...	576,954	140,377
" " " females .	203,622	21,360
Annual wages	195,976,453	33,257,560
" products..................	842,586,058	165,413,027
" profit.....................	376,741,966	79,222,388
" profit per cent..............	42	44
" wages per hand, males and females..............	251	206
" product " " "	1,079	1,029
" profit " " "	484	489

From this aggregate of Southern manufactures should be deducted the manufactures of certain counties where there is a large or predominating free population born out of the limits of

TABLE XIX.

A Statement of the Number of Individuals and Establishments engaged in Manufactures, the Amount of Capital invested in such Establishments, the Value of the Raw Material used, the Number of Hands employed, the Annual Wages paid, the Annual Product and the Annual Profit of such Manufactures, in the several Free States, according to the Census Returns of 1850.

FREE STATES.	Number of Individuals and Establishments.	Capital.	Value of Raw Material used.	Hands Employed. Male.	Female.	Annual Wages.	Annual Product.	Annual Profit, according to De Bow.
California.........	1,003	$1,006,197	$1,201,154	3,964		$3,485,820	$12,862,522	$11,661,368
Connecticut	3,482	23,890,348	23,589,397	31,287	16,483	11,695,236	45,110,102	21,520,705
Illinois	3,164	6,385,387	8,915,173	11,632	433	3,826,249	17,236,073	8,320,900
Indiana	4,288	7,941,602	10,214,337	13,677	665	2,809,116	18,922,651	8,708,314
Iowa...........	522	1,292,875	2,356,881	1,687	20	473,016	3,551,783	1,194,902
Maine	3,977	14,700,452	13,555,806	21,856	6,222	7,502,916	24,664,135	11,108,329
Massachusetts ...	8,259	83,357,642	85,856,771	96,261	69,677	39,784,116	151,137,145	65,280,374
Michigan	1,963	6,534,250	6,105,561	8,930	360	2,387,928	10,976,894	4,871,333
New Hampshire ..	3,211	18,242,114	12,745,466	14,103	12,989	6,123,876	23,164,503	10,419,037
New Jersey......	4,108	22,184,730	21,992,186	28,549	8,762	9,202,788	39,713,586	17,721,400
New York	23,553	99,904,405	134,655,674	147,737	51,612	49,131,000	237,597,249	102,941,575
Ohio	10,622	29,019,538	34,677,937	47,054	4,435	13,467,660	62,647,259	27,969,322
Pennsylvania....	21,605	94,473,810	87,206,377	124,688	22,078	37,163,232	155,044,910	67,838,533
Rhode Island ...	853	12,923,176	13,183,889	12,837	8,044	5,008,656	22,093,258	8,909,369
Vermont	1,849	5,001,377	4,172,552	6,894	1,551	2,202,348	8,570,920	4,398,368
Wisconsin.......	1,262	3,382,148	5,414,931	5,798	291	1,712,496	9,293,068	3,878,137
Total	93,721	$430,240,051	$465,844,092	576,954	203,622	$195,976,453	$942,586,058	$376,741,966

6

TABLE XX.

A Statement of the Number of Individuals and Establishments engaged in Manufactures, the Amount of Capital invested in such Establishments, the Value of the Raw Material used, the Number of Hands employed, the Annual Wages paid, the Annual Product and the Annual Profit of such Manufactures, in the several Slave States, according to the Census Returns of 1850.

SLAVE STATES.	Number of Individuals and Establishments.	Capital.	Value of Raw Material used.	Hands Employed.		Annual Wages.	Annual Product.	Annual Profit, according to De Bow.
				Male.	Female.			
Alabama	1,026	$3,450,606	$2,224,960	4,399	539	$1,106,112	$4,538,878	$2,313,918
Arkansas	272	324,065	268,564	873	30	169,356	607,436	338,872
Delaware	531	2,978,945	2,864,607	3,227	651	936,924	4,649,296	1,784,689
Florida	103	547,060	220,611	876	115	199,452	668,335	447,724
Georgia	1,527	5,460,483	3,404,917	6,660	1,718	1,712,304	7,086,525	3,681,608
Kentucky	3,609	12,350,734	12,170,225	22,445	1,940	4,764,096	24,588,483	12,418,258
Louisiana	1,017	5,318,074	2,958,988	5,581	856	2,086,212	7,320,948	4,361,960
Maryland	3,708	14,753,143	17,326,734	22,641	7,483	7,374,672	32,477,702	15,140,968
Mississippi	877	1,833,420	1,290,271	3,065	108	775,128	2,972,038	1,682,767
Missouri	3,029	9,079,695	12,446,738	15,997	873	3,184,764	23,749,265	11,302,527
North Carolina	2,604	7,252,225	4,805,463	10,693	1,751	1,796,748	9,111,245	4,305,782
South Carolina	1,431	6,056,865	2,809,534	5,935	1,074	1,128,432	7,063,513	4,253,979
Tennessee	2,861	6,975,279	4,900,952	11,154	878	2,277,228	9,728,438	4,827,486
Texas	309	539,290	394,642	1,042	24	322,368	1,165,538	770,896
Virginia	4,741	18,109,993	18,103,433	25,789	3,320	5,413,764	29,705,387	11,601,954
Total	27,645	$95,029,879	$86,190,639	140,377	21,360	$33,257,560	$165,413,027	$79,222,388

the several States in which the counties are situated. The
amount of the manufactures, and the character of the population, as regards birth, of the most important of these counties,
is shown in the following table. Even this deduction leaves
too large a balance for Southern manufactures, proper, for
everywhere throughout the South the most thriving manufactures were founded, or are sustained, by Northern capital, skill,
or labor.

TABLE XXI.

*A Statement of the Number of Free Inhabitants born within and without cer-
tain Counties of the Slave States, in which there is a large or predominating
exotic Population, with the Amount of Capital invested in Manufactures,
Number of Hands Employed, and the Annual Product thereof in 1850.*

COUNTIES.	Free Popula- tion born out of the State in which each Co. is situated.	Do. born in the State.	Capital.	Hands Em- ployed.	Annual Product.
Newcastle, Del...............	13,801	28,555	$2,593,830	3,235	$3,945,399
Baltimore, Md...............	61,472	142,456	9,929,332	23,863	24,540,014
Ohio, Va.....................	9,020	8,822	1,184,111	2,493	2,401,434
Charleston, S. C.............	7,844	21,225	1,487,800	1,413	2,749,961
Muscogee, Geo...............	2,589	7,838	713,217	719	788,580
Richmond, Geo..............	3,252	5,183	775,600	995	1,020,651
Mobile, Ala.................	10,379	7,865	522,800	540	1,261,450
Orleans, La.................	68,525	32,867	2,969,660	3,134	4,470,454
Galveston, Texas............	2,907	908	46,450	131	207,100
Davidson, Tenn..............	7,716	16,991	855,015	1,219	1,075,287
Shelby, Tenn................	9,077	7,720	424,130	789	840,789
Jefferson, Ky................	30,174	18,746	4,115,582	8,865	11,002,103
St. Louis, Mo...............	71,617	27,394	5,215,716	10,239	16,046,521
Total......................	298,373	326,565	$30,833,143	57,636	$70,296,743

This table includes the counties in which are situated the
cities of Baltimore, Wheeling, Louisville, St. Louis, New
Orleans, Mobile, Charleston, and some others. It will be
seen that, in these counties, the free population born within
and without the limits of each State, respectively, is nearly
equal. The manufacturing establishments in these counties
are generally confined to their cities, and a table showing
the origin of the free population of the cities only, would give

a large preponderance of persons born without the limits of their respective States. The means of constructing such a table are not accessible. There are, besides, other counties of smaller size which should be included with those in the foregoing table. These are necessarily omitted.

Deducting the aggregates of this table from the total manufactures reported for the South, and there are left for the manufactures of the Slave States,

Capital, ... $64,196,736
Hands employed, males and females, 104,101
Annual product, ... $95,116,284
Annual product per head, . . . 914

Adding the aggregates of table XXI. to those reported above for the manufactures of the North, and the total manufactures of the free population of the United States, will be :

Capital, ... $461,073,194
Hands employed, males and females, 838,212
Annual product, ... $912,882,801
Annual product per head, . . 1,089

Further amendment of these aggregates should be made by adding for California — in which State the marshal's returns for 1850 were generally defective, and for the most important localities lost or destroyed by fire — the following estimates, based on the returns of the State census for that State, taken in 1852, and ordered by Congress to be made a part of the National census, viz :

Capital, ... $5,942,526
Annual product, ... 30,000,000

The true total, then, of the manufactures of the free population of the United States for 1850 will be :

Capital invested, ... $467,015,720
Hands employed, males and females, 838,212
Annual product, ... $942,882,801

Thus, then, in seven times the capital invested, in eight

times the number of hands employed, in ten times the annual product, is the triumph of freedom over slavery seen in the department of manufactures. And this, after allowing to slavery millions of the capital of the North, thousands of its intelligent mechanics and operatives, and hundreds of its inventions and improvements, scattered throughout the South, wherever machinery is in motion, or labor skillfully applied to it. And this stagnation and sleep of slavery beneath the thundering of its thousands of waterfalls, and beside its millions of cotton bales.

Well did Governor Wise say to the Virginians: "You have the line of the Alleghanies, that beautiful ridge which stands placed there by the Almighty, not to obstruct the way of people to market, but placed there in the very bounty of Providence, to milk the clouds, to make the sweet springs which are the sources of your rivers. And at the head of every stream is the waterfall, murmuring the very music of your power. And yet commerce has long ago spread her sails and sailed away from you; you have not as yet dug more than coal enough to warm yourselves at your own hearths; you have no tilt-hammer of Vulcan, to strike blows worthy of gods in the iron foundries. You have not yet spun more than coarse cotton enough to clothe your own slaves. You have had no commerce, no mining, no manufactures." (Speech at Alexandria, 1855.)

Table XXII. contains a list of those counties in the Free and Slave States which had, in 1850, the greatest relative amount of manufactures. The areas given are from Baldwin and Thomas' Gazetteer of 1854; the value of the land is ascertained by dividing the value given in the Census Compendium by the whole area. The Southern counties taken are such as have no large admixture of exotic population. In these counties are included the important cities of Wilmington, N. C., Lynchburg, Va., and Clarksville, Tenn.

6*

TABLE XXII.

Counties in the Free and Slave States which had, in 1850, the greatest relative Amount of Manufactures.

Counties in Free States.	Area in Square Miles.	Population.	Value of Farms.	Annual Product of Manufactories.	Value of Land per Acre.	Average Product of Manufactures per head of whole population.
Bristol, Mass....	517	76,192	$7,101,582	$12,595,695	$21.46	$165
Essex, Mass.....	500	131,300	9,582,992	22,906,805	29.95	174
Middlesex, Mass.	830	161,383	19,417,796	26,548,932	36.55	164
Norfolk, Mass....	520	78,892	13,748,505	13,323,595	41.31	169
Kent, R. I.......	180	15,068	1,951,111	2,620,788	17.80	174
Hartford, Conn..	807	69,967	14,004,683	10,888,780	27.12	156
N. Haven, Conn..	620	65,588	10,413,662	11,283,816	26.24	172
Essex, N. J......	450	73,950	7,219,566	16,293,198	25.07	220
Passaic, N. J.....	270	22,569	3,302,051	4,213,699	19.11	187
Total...........	4,684	694,909	$86,741,948	$120,675,308	$28.94	$174
Counties in Slaves States.						
Campbell, Va....	576	23,245	$2,452,604	$1,839,307	$6.65	$79
N. Hanover, N.C.	1,000	17,668	1,035,874	1,409,568	1.62	80
M'tgomery, Ten.	550	21,045	1,359,836	1,376,300	3.86	65
Total...........	2,126	61,958	$4,848,314	$4,625,175	$3.56	$74

Tables **XXIII.** and **XXIV.** show the value of the manufactures of cotton, wool, iron, the fisheries, and salt, in 1850. It is to be regretted that the returns of the details of the other branches of manufactures have not yet been published by Congress. These tables will repay a careful examination.

Table **XXV.** gives the value of the domestic manufactures in the several Free and Slave States, for the year ending June, 1850; and gives also the annual increase of slaves in the several Slave States, with their value at $400 per head. It is to be understood that a larger proportion of slaves is born in the slave-raising States, and a smaller in the slave-consuming States, than is shown by the tables. As to this product of Southern labor, or skill, or necessity — the annual slave product — it may be classed indifferently under the head of agriculture, manufactures, or commerce. As live

TABLE XXIII.

A Statement of the Value of the Manufactures of Cotton, Wool, Pig Iron, Iron Castings, Wrought Iron, and of the Products of the Fisheries and Salt Manufactures, in the several Free States, for the year ending June, 1850, with the average Wages per month of the Hands employed.

FREE STATES	Value of Cotton Manufactures.	Value of Woollen Manufactures.	Value of Manufactures of Pig Iron.	Value of Manufactures of Iron Casting.	Value of Manufactures of Wrought Iron.	Value of Products of the Fisheries.	Value of Salt Manufactures.	Wages per month in Cotton Manufactures. — Males.	Wages per month in Cotton Manufactures. — Females.	Wages per month in Woollen Manufactures. — Males.	Wages per month in Woollen Manufactures. — Females.	Wages per month in Manufactures of Pig Iron. — Males.	Wages per month in Manufactures of Iron Casting. — Males.
California				$20,740									$23.33
Connecticut	$4,257,522	$6,465,216	$415,600	981,400	$847,196	$1,734,483	$5,600	$19.08	$11.80	$24.12	$12.86	$26.80	27.02
Illinois		206,572	70,200	441,185			6,000			21.81	12.52	22.06	28.50
Indiana	44,200	205,802	58,000	149,430	11,760			13.02	6.77	11.14	11.05	26.00	25.74
Iowa		13,000		8,500						22.57	11.77		32.35
Maine	2,596,356	753,300	36,616	265,000		569,876	9,700	29.35	12.15	22.95	14.22	22.00	29.00
Massachusetts	19,712,461	12,770,565	295,123	2,235,635	3,908,952	6,606,849	93,850	22.90	13.60	21.65	11.47	27.52	30.90
Michigan		90,242	21,000	279,697	20,400	72,775				22.86	14.53	35.00	28.68
New Hampshire	8,830,619	2,127,745	6,000	371,710	1,079,576	59,281		26.00	13.47	25.22	8.60	18.00	33.05
New Jersey	1,164,524	1,164,446	560,544	686,430	3,758,547			17.98	9.56	19.97	11.76	21.20	24.00
New York	3,591,989	7,030,604	597,920	5,921,980	127,849	484,345	998,315	18.32	9.68	20.14	10.90	25.00	27.49
Ohio	394,700	1,111,027	1,255,850	3,069,350	9,224,256	27,565	132,293	16.59	9.42	19.43	10.41	24.48	27.32
Pennsylvania	5,322,262	5,321,866	6,071,513	5,354,881	223,650		206,796	17.85	9.91	20.70	15.18	21.65	27.55
Rhode Island	6,447,120	2,381,825		728,705		64,430		18.60	12.95	24.46	11.81		29.63
Vermont	196,100	1,579,161	68,000	460,831	127,886			15.53	12.65	22.48		22.08	28.27
Wisconsin		87,992	27,000	216,195		16,875						30.00	26.73
Total	$52,502,853	$41,309,363	$9,483,366	$21,191,669	$19,330,072	$9,636,479	$1,452,554						

TABLE XXIV.

A Statement of the Value of the Manufactures of Cotton, Wool, Pig Iron, Iron Castings, Wrought Iron, and of the Products of the Fisheries and Salt Manufactories, of the several Slave States, for the year ending June, 1850, with the average Wages per month of the Hands employed.

SLAVE STATES.	Value of Cotton Manufactures.	Value of Woollen Manufactures.	Value of Manufactures of Pig Iron.	Value of Manufactures of Iron Casting.	Value of Manufactures of Wrought Iron.	Value of products of the Fisheries.	Value of Salt Manufactures.	Wages per month in Cotton Manufactures. Males.	Wages per month in Cotton Manufactures. Females.	Wages per month in Woollen Manufactures. Males.	Wages per month in Woollen Manufactures. Females.	Wages per month in Manufactures of Iron Casting.—Males.	Wages per month in Manufactures of Pig Iron.—Males.
Alabama	$332,260	....	$22,500	$271,126	$7,500	....	....	$11.71	$7.98	....	....	$17.60	$30.05
Arkansas	16,637	....	....	....	....	....	....	14.61	5.88	....	....	....	....
Delaware	533,439	$251,000	....	267,462	38,200	....	....	15.31	11.58	$18.79	$17.33	20.14	23.86
Maryland	2,120,504	295,140	1,056,400	685,000	771,431	$18,676	$6,000	15.42	9.42	18.60	11.89	....	27.50
Florida	49,920	....	....	....	....	....	....	32.14	5.00	....	....	....	....
Georgia	2,135,044	88,750	57,300	46,200	12,384	....	....	14.57	7.39	27.47	14.10	17.44	27.43
Kentucky	273,439	318,819	604,037	744,316	299,700	....	57,825	14.95	9.36	15.30	11.11	20.23	24.89
Louisiana	....	....	....	312,500	....	....	....	....	....	....	....	....	35.60
Mississippi	30,500	....	....	117,400	....	....	....	14.21	5.94	....	....	....	37.91
Missouri	142,900	56,000	314,600	336,495	68,700	....	....	10.93	10.00	32.00	6.50	24.28	19.63
North Carolina	831,842	23,750	12,500	12,867	331,914	250,025	....	11.65	6.13	18.00	7.00	8.00	23.46
South Carolina	748,338	....	....	87,683	....	....	....	13.94	8.30	....	....	....	13.59
Tennessee	510,624	6,310	576,100	264,325	670,618	....	5,900	10.94	6.42	17.66	6.00	12.81	17.96
Texas	....	15,000	....	55,000	....	....	....	....	....	20.00	20.00	....	43.43
Virginia	1,486,384	841,013	521,924	674,416	1,098,252	95,002	700,466	10.18	6.98	18.17	9.91	12.76	19.91
Total	$9,266,331	$1,895,782	$3,264,961	$3,874,790	$3,298,699	$363,703	$770,191						

TABLE XXV.

A Statement of the Value of the Domestic Manufactures of the several Free and Slave States for the years 1850; *with the average Annual Increase, and Value at* $400 *per head, of Slaves, for the ten years ending June,* 1850.

FREE STATES.	Value of Domestic Manufactures for 1850.	SLAVE STATES.	Value of Domestic Manufactures for 1850.	Annual Increase of Slaves from 1840 to 1850.	Value at $400 per head.
California.....	$7,000	Alabama	$1,934,120	8,931	$3,572,400
Connecticut...	192,252	Arkansas	938,217	2,717	1,086,800
Illinois	1,155,902	Delaware......	38,121	31	12,400
Indiana.......	1,631,039	Florida........	75,582	1,359	543,600
Iowa	221,292	Georgia	1,838,968	10,074	4,029,600
Maine	513,599	Kentucky.....	2,459,128	2,872	1,148,800
Massachusetts.	205,333	Louisiana	139,232	7,636	3,054,400
Michigan	340,947	Maryland	111,828	63	25,200
N. Hampshire.	393,455	Mississippi	1,164,020	11,467	4,586,800
New Jersey ...	112,781	Missouri	1,674,705	2,918	1,167,200
New York.....	1,280,333	North Carolina	2,086,522	4,273	1,709,200
Ohio..........	1,712,196	South Carolina	909,525	5,795	2,318,000
Pennsylvania .	749,132	Tennessee.....	3,137,790	5,640	2,256,000
Rhode Island..	26,495	Texas.........	266,984	5,816	2,326,400
Vermont......	267,710	Virginia	2,156,312	2,344	937,600
Wisconsin	43,624	....	....	....	....
Total.........	$8,853,090	Total	$18,631,054	71,936	$28,774,400

stock raised and fattened for market, it would seem to belong legitimately to the department of agriculture; as an article of trade, to commerce; but a better arrangement is to class it with domestic manufactures, that class of manufactures in which it will be seen that the South is ahead. In this work, then, the slave product is classed with domestic manufactures, and its value — no estimate having been made by De Bow — computed from the best authorities, will be included in the aggregates for that branch of manufactures. The number of slaves annually manufactured by the Northern Slave States for the Southern markets is given elsewhere as 25,000; their value at $400 per head is $10,000,000. This is a small estimate both as to number and value. As to the capital invested, the value of the raw material used, the number of hands employed, and the annual wages paid in this species of manufacture, the census tables give no information.

CHAPTER VI.

COMMERCE.

IT is difficult to apportion the results of commerce to the several States. The statistics of the great branch of domestic or internal commerce are very incomplete; the returns of the minor branch of foreign or external commerce are more full. De Bow suggests that "half the agricultural products and all of the manufacturing are subjects of commerce, and that the whole commercial movement may be estimated at between $1,500,000,000 and $2,000,000,000 " annually. Adopting this suggestion, the value of the products which enter into the commerce of the two sections, for 1850, would be as follows, viz:

Free States, ...	$1,377,199,968
Slave States, ...	410,754,992
Total, ...	$1,787,954,960

No enumeration, by States, of the persons engaged in commerce, trade, and navigation, is given in the Compendium of the Census of 1850. In 1840, however, such enumeration was made, and is found in the published census returns for that year. The number of persons engaged in commerce, navigating the ocean, and in internal navigation, was in 1840 as follows, viz:

Free States, ...	136,856
Slave States, ...	52,622
Total, ...	189,478

This would give, in 1850, as the number of persons engaged in commerce and navigation, —

Free States, ... 188,271
Slave States, ... 70,165
                                 ———————
Total, ... 258,436

Domestic commerce is carried on by the enrolled and licensed tonnage (with the participation, in a small proportion, of the registered), by railroads, canals, and public roads. Of enrolled and licensed tonnage, there were in 1850, in the

Free States, ... 1,459,232 tons.
Slave States, ... 475,405 "
                                 ———————
Total, . . . : . . 1,934,637 "

Of railroads in operation in 1854, there were, miles, in the

Free States, ... 13,105
Slave States, ... 4,212
                                 ———————
Total, ... 17,317

Of canals, there were in 1854, miles, in the

Free States, ... 3,682
Slave States, ... 1,116
                                 ———————
Total, ... 4,798

There are no statistics of the miles of public roads in the two sections, or of the merchandise and produce transported over them.

We may be aided in forming an estimate of the amount of our domestic commerce, by the following tabular statements, from Andrews' report:

TABLE XXVI.

Lake and River Commerce.

1851.	Net.		Gross.	
	Tons.	Value.	Tons.	Value.
Lake Commerce........................	1,985,563	$157,236,729	3,971,126	$314,473,458
River Commerce......................	2,033,400	169,751,372	4,066,800	339,502,744
Aggregate...........................	4,018,963	$326,988,101	8,037,926	$653,976,202

Coasting Trade, Canal and Railway Commerce.

Estimate of 1852.	Net.		Gross.	
	Tons.	Value.	Tons.	Value.
Coasting trade.............	20,397,490	$1,659,519,686	40,794,980	$3,319,039,372
Canal Commerce..........	9,000,000	594,000,000	18,000,000	1,188,000,000
Railway Commerce........	5,407,500	540,750,000	10,815,000	1,081,500,000
Aggregate................	34,804,990	$2,794,269,686	69,609,980	$5,588,539,372

It is estimated by Andrews that the number of tons of shipping engaged in the coasting trade is 2,039,749.

This is the amount of the "enrolled and licensed tonnage." In addition, considerable "registered tonnage" frequently enters the coasting trade between the Atlantic ports and those on the Gulf and the Pacific.

The "licensed tonnage" engaged in the lake commerce is 215,975 tons. The tonnage engaged in the river commerce is 169,450 tons. The foregoing figures are for the years 1851 and 1852.

In a late report of the Committee on Commerce, it is stated that, "The lake tonnage for 1855 was 345,000 tons, which, valued at $45 per ton, is $14,838,000. The present value of lake commerce (exclusive of the ports of Presque Isle and Mackinac, not reported) is $608,310,320."

Our foreign commerce is carried on by the registered tonnage of the United States, and by the tonnage of other nations. The foreign tonnage which entered the ports of the United States, in 1851, was 1,939,091 tons; the American tonnage, 3,054,349 tons. De Bow says, of 1851, that the value of merchandise imported in "foreign vessels was $52,563,083; in American vessels $168,216,272." By this, it will be seen that something more than three-fourths of the value of our foreign commerce is carried on in American vessels. The registered tonnage of the two sections, in 1850 was, in the

Free States,	.	.	.	.	. 1,330,963 tons.
Slave States,	.	.	.	.	. 250,880 "
Total,	.	.	.	.	. 1,581,843 "

We may now approximate the truth in regard to the commerce of the two sections of our country in three ways.

First. Taking the value of the products which enter into commerce, we find the North has $1,377,199,968; the South $410,754,992, giving the North more than three to one.

Second. Taking the number of persons engaged in trade, and the North has 188,271 persons, the South 70,165 persons, giving the North nearly three to one, and this on the supposition that the average amount of business done by merchants in the South is as great as in the North.

Third. Taking the tonnage, miles of railroads, and canals: the North had, in 1850, 2,790,195 tons of registered, enrolled and licensed tonnage, the South 726,285 tons. (The amount of tonnage in 1855 was, in the North 4,252,615 tons, in the South 855,517 tons.) The North had in 1854, 13,105 miles of railroad in operation, the South 4,212 miles. The North had in the same year 3,682 miles of canals, the South 1,116 miles. This gives a ratio of something more than three to one in favor of the North. It may, we think, be fairly assumed that the amount of commerce and its profits in the two sections are quite four times as much in the North as in the South.

We have thus shown, from such data as could be obtained, the relative proportion of the domestic and foreign commerce of the Free and Slave States. Adopting the suggestion of De Bow (as to the value of the "commercial movement"), the domestic commerce of the United States, in 1850, was six times that of the foreign. The figures are as follows:

Value of manufactures and half of agricultual
  products, ... $1,787,954,960
Value of imports, ... 178,078,499
  Total, ... 1,966,033,459
Total value of imports and exports, . . 329,896,631

Adopting the estimates of Andrews (Report on Lake Commerce), the domestic commerce of the United States, in 1851–2, was nearly eight times the foreign. The figures are as follows, viz:

Value of lake and river commerce, . . $326,988,101
Value of coasting trade, railway and canal
  commerce, ... 2,794,269,686
Value of imports, 1851, ... 216,224,932
  Total, ... 3,337,482,719
Total value of imports and exports, 1851, . 434,612,943

It is, perhaps, not far from right to call the domestic commerce of this country seven times the foreign.

Tables XXVII. and XXVIII. give the value of the exports and imports of the several Free and Slave States for 1850 and 1855; and the amount and value of tonnage owned and built in the same years. The tables are compiled from the annual report on commerce and navigation. The statistics of exports and imports show the *foreign commerce* of the several States. The aggregates for the two years given are —

Free States, ... $631,396,034
Slave States, ... 234,936,306
                                    ————————
  Total, ... $866,332,340

being nearly three times as much in the North as in the South.

TABLE XXVII.

A Statement of the Value of the Exports and Imports of the Several Free States, for the years ending June 30, 1850, and June 30, 1855, with the Tonnage owned in said States at those dates, and the Tonnage built therein during said years, with its Value.

FREE STATES.	Value of Exports for the year ending June 30, 1850.	Value of Imports for the year ending June 30, 1850.	Value of Exports for the year ending June 30, 1855.	Value of Imports for the year ending June 30, 1855.	Tonnage owned June 30, 1850.	Value at $50 per ton.	Tonnage built for the year ending June 30, 1850.	Value at $50 per ton.	Tonnage owned June 30, 1855.	Value at $50 per ton.	Tonnage built for the year ending June 30, 1855.	Value at $50 per ton.
Maine	$1,553,912	$856,411	$4,851,207	$2,927,443	501,422	$25,071,100	91,212	$4,560,600	806,587	$40,329,350	215,905	$10,795,250
N. Hampshire	8,927	49,079	1,523	17,786	23,096	1,154,800	6,914	345,700	30,330	1,516,500	8,928	496,400
Vermont	430,906	463,092	2,895,468	591,593	4,530	226,500	77	3,850	6,915	345,750	none.	....
Massachusetts	10,681,763	30,874,684	28,190,925	45,113,774	685,442	34,272,100	35,836	1,791,800	970,727	48,536,350	79,670	3,983,500
Rhode Island	216,265	258,308	336,023	536,387	40,489	2,024,450	3,587	179,350	51,038	2,551,900	7,862	393,100
Connecticut	241,930	372,390	878,874	636,826	113,087	5,654,350	4,820	241,000	137,170	6,858,500	14,067	703,350
New York	52,712,789	111,123,524	113,731,238	164,776,511	944,349	47,217,450	58,342	2,917,100	1,404,221	70,211,050	115,231	5,761,550
New Jersey	1,655	1,494	687	1,473	80,300	4,015,000	6,202	310,100	121,020	6,051,000	10,960	548,000
Pennsylvania	4,501,606	12,066,154	6,274,338	15,309,935	258,039	12,901,950	21,410	1,070,500	397,768	19,888,400	44,415	2,220,750
Ohio	217,632	582,504	847,143	600,656	62,462	3,123,100	5,215	260,750	91,607	4,580,350	17,751	887,550
Michigan	182,045	144,102	568,091	281,379	38,145	1,907,250	2,062	103,100	69,490	3,474,500	7,844	392,200
Wisconsin	....	....	174,057	48,159	....	....	....	....	15,624	781,200	1,452	72,600
Illinois	17,669	15,705	547,053	54,509	21,242	1,062,100	1,691	84,550	53,797	2,689,850	1,903	95,150
California	....	....	8,224,066	5,951,879	17,592	879,600	....	....	92,623	4,631,150	2,118	105,900
Indiana	....	....	....	....	....	....	....	....	3,698	184,900	738	36,900
Total	$70,720,099	$156,307,442	$167,520,693	$236,847,810	2,790,195	$189,509,750	237,368	$11,868,400	4,252,615	$212,630,750	528,844	$26,442,200

TABLE XXVIII.

A Statement of the Value of the Exports and Imports of the several Slave States for the years 1850 and 1855, and of the Tonnage owned in said States on the 30th of June, 1850 and 1855, and of the Tonnage built therein for the years ending June 30, 1850, and June 30, 1855, with the Value of said Tonnage.

SLAVE STATES.	Value of Exports for the year ending June 30, 1850.	Value of Imports for the year ending June 30, 1850.	Value of Exports for the year ending June 30, 1855.	Value of Imports for the year ending June 30, 1855.	Tonnage owned June 30, 1850.	Value at $50 per ton.	Tonnage built for the year ending June 30, 1850.	Value at per ton.	Tonnage owned June 30, 1855.	Value at $50 per ton.	Tonnage built for the year ending June 30, 1855.	Value at $50 per ton.
Delaware			$68,087	$5,821	16,720	$836,000	1,849	$92,450	19,186	$959,300	5,488	$274,400
Maryland	$6,967,353	$6,124,201	10,395,984	7,788,949	193,087	9,654,350	15,965	798,250	234,805	11,740,250	22,534	1,126,700
Virginia	3,415,646	426,599	4,379,928	865,405	74,071	3,703,550	3,584	179,200	92,788	4,639,400	4,603	230,150
North Carolina	416,501	323,692	433,818	243,083	45,219	2,261,950	2,652	132,600	60,077	3,003,850	2,595	129,750
South Carolina	11,447,800	1,933,785	12,700,250	1,588,542	36,072	1,803,600			60,935	3,046,750	61	3,050
Georgia	7,551,943	635,964	7,543,519	273,716	21,690	1,084,500	684	34,200	29,505	1,475,250	195	9,750
Florida	2,623,624	95,709	1,403,594	45,998	11,273	563,650	80	4,000	14,835	741,750	275	13,750
Alabama	10,544,858	865,362	14,270,685	619,964	24,158	1,207,900	114	5,700	36,274	1,813,700	669	33,450
Louisiana	38,105,350	10,760,419	55,367,962	12,900,821	250,090	12,504,500	1,592	79,600	204,149	10,207,450	872	43,600
Mississippi				1,661	1,828	91,400			2,475	123,750	370	18,500
Tennessee		27,966			3,776	188,800			8,404	420,200	428	21,400
Missouri		359,643			20,908	1,445,400	1,354	67,700	60,592	3,029,600	5,084	254,200
Kentucky		190,987			14,820	741,000	6,461	323,050	22,680	1,134,000	9,401	470,050
Texas	24,958	25,650	916,961	262,568	4,573	228,650	106	5,300	8,812	440,600	324	16,200
Total	$81,098,033	$21,771,057	$107,480,688	$24,586,528	726,285	$36,314,250	34,441	$1,722,050	855,517	$42,775,850	52,959	$2,647,950

The tonnage of the two sections in 1855 was as follows, viz.

Free States, ...	4,252,015	tons.
Slave States, ...	855,517	"
Total, ...	5,108,132	"

being five times as much in the North as in the South.

The foreign commerce of New York alone, for 1855, was as follows, viz:

Exports, ...	$113,731,238
Imports, ...	164,776,511
Total, ...	$278,507,749

The foreign commerce of the Slave States for 1855 was as follows, viz:

Exports, ...	$107,480,688
Imports, ...	24,586,528
Total, ...	$132,067,216

This statement shows that the foreign commerce of New York, in 1855, was more than twice that of all the Slave States.

The tonnage of New York in 1855 was	1,404,221 tons.
The tonnage of the Slave States for the same year, ...	855,517 "
Or a little more than half that of the State of New York.	

The foreign commerce of Massachusetts and South Carolina, for 1855, was as follows, viz:

MASSACHUSETTS.

Exports, ...	$28,190,925
Imports, ...	45,113,774
Total, ...	$73,304,699

7*

SOUTH CAROLINA.

Exports, ...	$12,700,250
Imports, ...	1,588,542
Total, ...	$14,288,792

The tonnage of Massachusetts, in 1855, was . . . . 970,727 tons.

The tonnage of South Carolina for the same year was . . . . 60,935 "

The tonnage built in Massachusetts, in 1855, was 79,670 tons, valued at $3,983,500; the tonnage built in South Carolina in the same year, was 61 tons, valued at $3,050.

It will be observed by Tables XXVII. and XXVIII. that the large States of Indiana, Tennessee, Kentucky, and Missouri have no foreign commerce, and that the States of New Hampshire, New Jersey, Mississippi, and Delaware have very little.

The tonnage built in 1855 was as follows, viz:

Free States, ...	528,844 tons.
Slave States, ...	52,959 "
Total, ...	581,803 "

The North, therefore, builds of tonnage ten times as much as the South. In 1855, the tonnage built in the State of Maine was more than four times that built in the South; Maine having built 215,905 tons, the Slave States 52,959 tons. Of the tonnage built in the South, more than four-fifths of it is built in ports where there is a large or predominating free population, born out of the limits of the States in which such ports are respectively situated, as in Baltimore, St. Louis, Louisville, Wheeling, etc. Making a proper deduction for this, and the amount of shipping annually built by the Slave States will not exceed 10,000 tons. Even this small amount is not the work of slaveholders, or slaves, or of the poor whites of the South, but of northern and foreign-born mechanics and ship carpenters. In case of a dissolution of the Union, and hostilities between the North and South, the highest naval science would need to be called into requisition by the South, so to station this naval armament of sloops, schooners, and steamboats as to command her seven thousand miles of exposed sea and gulf-coast.

We close what we have to say on commerce, with the following extract from a letter of Mr. London, of Richmond, Va., to the Richmond Enquirer, and published in that paper early in 1854, just before the sitting of a Southern commercial convention at Charleston, S. C. He had been alluding to the sittings of other Southern commercial conventions at Memphis and elsewhere:

" We have, since that time, appropriated millions of dollars to works of internal improvement; some of us have embarked more largely in foreign trade; but *there are not half a dozen vessels engaged in our own trade that are owned in Virginia, and I have been unable to find a vessel at Liverpool loading for Virginia, within three years, during the height of our busy season.* Every foot of railroad and every yard of canal constructed in the Southern States *is only so much added to the area of the influence of New York, and but binds you that much more securely to her bonds.* Instead of these immense improvements resulting in an enlargement of your foreign commerce, *it is but a contribution to your coasting trade,* and results in establishing the calculation as to how long it will take your shopkeepers to get *the productions and importations of New York into your villages;* all else but this is not considered. As to any one of your improvements contributing to forward your own importations, *that is not thought of at all by your interior shopkeepers; for, throughout the South, all merchants have disappeared, entirely and completely.*"

CHAPTER VII.

VALUE OF REAL AND PERSONAL ESTATE.

TABLES XXIX, and XXX. give the value of the real and personal estate of the several States in 1850, according to the published census returns; the true value of the same as estimated by the superintendent of the census; the value of the slaves in the Slave States at $400 per head; and the value of the real and personal estate in 1856, as given by the Secretary of the Treasury in a communication to Congress at its late session. The estimate of $400 per head for slaves is, perhaps, too low. With a single apparent exception, the value of slaves is included by the compiler of the census returns in the value of personal estate. The exception is the State of Louisiana, in which State the value of the slaves is included in the value of real estate. With reference to the estimates of Mr. Secretary Guthrie, for Texas, it is hardly probable that its taxable property has gone up, in five years, from $55,362,340 to $240,000,000, an increase of about $200,000,000; while Iowa, which has increased in population since 1850 faster than any other State, is allowed an increase in taxable property of only $86,285,362, and Wisconsin of only $45,443,405. The valuation of Georgia is given by the secretary, not from the State valuation, but from an estimate of the governor of that State. The estimate for California is evidently too low, and is not according to any State valuation. In the case of Indiana, whose auditor, as quoted by Mr. Guthrie, says that a valuation at that time (November 24, 1855) would make the total taxables $380,000,000, the secretary, in 1856, gives the sum of $301,858,474, instead of the auditor's estimate,

TABLE XXIX.

A Statement of the Value of the Real and Personal Estate of the several Free States, and the True Value of the same in 1850; with the Value of the Real and Personal Estate of said States in 1856.

FREE STATES.	Value of Real Estate. 1850.	Value of Personal Estate. 1850.	Total Value of Real and Personal Estate. 1850.	True Value of Real and Personal Estate, as given in Census Compendium. 1850.	Value of Real and Personal Estate, as given by Secretary of Treasury. 1856.
California	$16,347,442	$5,575,731	$21,923,173	$22,161,872	$165,000,000
Connecticut	96,412,947	22,675,725	119,088,672	155,707,980	203,756,831
Illinois	81,524,835	33,257,810	114,782,645	156,265,006	333,237,474
Indiana	112,947,740	39,922,659	152,870,399	202,650,264	301,858,474
Iowa	15,672,332	6,018,310	21,690,642	23,714,638	110,000,000
Maine	64,336,119	32,463,434	96,799,553	122,777,571	131,128,186
Massachusetts	349,129,932	201,976,892	551,108,824	573,342,286	597,936,995
Michigan	25,580,371	5,296,852	30,877,223	59,787,255	116,593,580
New Hampshire	67,839,108	27,412,488	95,251,596	103,652,835	103,804,327
New Jersey	153,151,619	not returned.	153,151,619	153,151,619	179,750,000
New York	564,649,649	150,719,379	715,369,028	1,080,309,216	1,364,154,625
Ohio	337,521,075	96,351,557	433,872,632	504,726,120	860,877,354
Pennsylvania	427,865,660	72,410,191	500,275,851	729,144,998	1,031,731,304
Rhode Island	54,358,231	23,400,743	77,758,974	80,508,794	91,699,850
Vermont	57,320,369	15,660,114	72,980,483	92,205,049	91,165,680
Wisconsin	22,458,442	4,257,083	26,715,525	42,056,595	87,500,000
Total	$2,447,115,871	$737,398,768	$3,184,514,639	$4,102,162,198	$5,770,194,680

TABLE XXX.

A Statement of the Value of the Real and Personal Estate in 1850, of the True Value of the same, of the Value of the Slaves, of the True Value of the Real and Personal Estate, deducting the Value of the Slaves, with the Value of the Real and Personal Estate (including Slaves) for 1856, of the several Slave States.

SLAVE STATES.	Value of Real Estate. 1850.	Value of Personal Estate, including Slaves. 1850.	Total Value of Real and Personal Estate. 1850.	True Value of Real and Personal Estate, as given in Census Compendium. 1850.	Value of Slaves at $400 per head. 1850.	True Value of Real and Personal Estate, deducting the Value of Slaves, at $400 per head. 1850.	Value of Real and Personal Estate, as given by Secretary of Treasury. 1856.
Alabama	$78,870,718	$162,463,705	$241,334,423	$228,204,332	$137,187,600	$81,066,732	$279,233,027
Arkansas	17,372,524	19,056,151	36,428,675	39,841,025	18,840,000	21,001,025	64,240,726
Delaware	14,486,595	1,410,275	15,896,870	18,855,863	916,000	17,939,863	30,466,924
Florida	7,924,588	15,274,146	23,198,734	23,198,734	15,724,000	7,474,734	49,461,461
Georgia	121,619,739	213,490,486	335,110,225	335,425,714	152,672,800	182,752,914	500,000,000
Kentucky	177,013,407	114,374,147	291,387,554	301,628,456	84,392,400	217,236,056	411,000,098
Louisiana	176,726,654	49,882,464	226,456,118	233,998,764	97,923,600	136,075,164	270,425,000
Maryland	139,026,610	69,536,956	208,563,566	219,217,364	36,147,200	183,070,164	261,243,660
Mississippi	65,171,438	143,250,729	208,422,167	228,951,130	123,951,200	105,000,000	251,525,000
Missouri	66,802,223	31,793,240	98,595,463	137,247,707	34,968,800	102,278,907	223,948,781
North Carolina	71,702,740	140,368,673	212,071,413	226,800,472	115,419,200	111,381,272	239,603,372
South Carolina	105,787,492	178,130,217	283,867,709	288,257,694	153,993,600	134,264,094	303,434,240
Tennessee	107,981,793	87,299,565	195,281,358	207,454,704	95,783,600	111,671,104	321,776,810
Texas	28,149,671	25,414,000	53,563,671	55,362,340	23,264,400	32,097,940	240,000,000
Virginia	252,105,824	130,198,429	382,304,253	391,646,438	189,011,200	202,634,638	580,994,897
Total	$1,430,569,016	$1,381,894,183	$2,812,473,199	$2,986,090,737	$1,280,145,600	$1,655,945,137	$3,977,353,946

and this after having added to the valuation of Georgia $165,000,000, on the bare conjecture of her governor.

The following recent State valuations will further illustrate the estimates of the Secretary of the Treasury:

Valuation of New Hampshire, 1856, . .	$121,417,428
" " New York, 1855, as follows, viz:	
New York city and county real estate, .	337,038,526
" " " personal estate, .	150,022,312
" " " aggregate, . .	487,060,838
Remainder of State real estate, . . .	770,234,189
" " personal estate, . .	143,990,252
Total valuation of the State of New York, .	1,401,285,279
Valuation of New York city, 1856, . .	517,889,201
" " Connecticut, 1854, . .	202,739,431
" " Michigan, 1853, . .	120,362,474
" " Indiana, 1854, . .	290,408,148
" " Maryland, including slaves, 1851,	191,888,088
" " South Carolina, " " 1854,	82,613,530
" " Tennessee, " " 1855,	219,011,048
" " Kentucky, " " 1854,	405,830,168

It will be seen by tables XXIX. and XXX. that the value of real and personal estate in 1850 was as follows, viz:

Free States, ...	$4,102,162,192
Slave States, ...	2,936,090,737
Deduct value of slaves, . .	1,280,145,600
True value in Slave States, . .	1,655,945,137

The total value of real and personal estate in 1856 is as follows, viz :

Free States, ...	$5,770,194,680
Slave States, ...	3,977,353,946
Deduct value of slaves in 1856, .	1,472,167,600
True value in Slave States in 1856,	2,505,186,346

The whole area of the Free States (Tables I. and IX.) is 392,-962,080 acres; the valuation of real and personal property in 1850, $4,107,162,198, or $10.47 per acre. The whole area (Table

X.) of the Slave States is five hundred and forty-four million, nine hundred and twenty-six thousand, seven hundred and twenty (544,926,720) acres; the valuation of real and personal estate in 1850, one billion, six hundred and fifty-five million, nine hundred and forty-five thousand, one hundred and thirty-seven ($1,655,945,137), or three dollars and four cents ($3.04) per acre. The valuation of the Free States in 1856 was five billion, seven hundred and seventy million, one hundred and ninety-four thousand, six hundred and eighty ($5,770,194,680), or fourteen dollars and seventy-two cents ($14.72) per acre; the valuation of the Slave States in 1856 was two billion, five hundred and five million, one hundred and eighty-six thousand, three hundred and forty-six ($2,505,186,346), or four dollars and fifty-nine cents ($4.59) per acre. Thus, in five years the value of property in the Free States advanced from ten dollars and forty-seven cents ($10.47) per acre to fourteen dollars and seventy-two cents ($14.72), or four dollars and twenty-five cents ($4.25), being more than the whole valuation of the Slave States in 1850. The value of property in the South advanced in the same time from three dollars and four cents ($3.04) to four dollars and fifty-nine cents ($4.59) per acre.

The value of the slaves in the Slave States, in 1850, at four hundred dollars ($400) each, was one billion two hundred and eighty million, one hundred and forty-five thousand, six hundred dollars ($1,280,145,600). The value of the farms in the Slave States in the same year (Table X.) was one billion, one hundred and seventeen million, six hundred and forty-nine thousand, six hundred and forty-nine dollars ($1,117,649,649). Excess of value of slaves, one hundred and sixty-two million, four hundred and ninety-five thousand, nine hundred and fifty-one dollars ($162,495,951). Thus, the value of the slaves in 1850 was one hundred and sixty-two million, four hundred and ninetyfive thousand, nine hundred and fifty-one dollars ($162,-495,951) more than the value of all the improved and unimproved lands in the South. The number of slaveholders in the Slave States is three hundred and forty-six thousand and forty-eight (346,048). If we estimate their value at four hundred dollars ($400) per head, and add it to the value of the farms, it will make the value of the slaveholders and farms nearly equal to that of the slaves. The figures are: Value of farms, one billion, one hundred and seventeen million, six hundred and forty-nine thousand, six hundred and forty-nine ($1,117,649,649); value of three hundred and forty-six thouand and forty-eight (346,048) slaveholders, at four hundred dollars ʹ$400) each, one hundred and thirty-eight million, one hundred and ninety-two thousand, two hundred dollars ($138,192,200), being a total of one billion, two hundred and fifty-six million, sixty-eight thousand, eight hundred and forty-nine dollars ($1,-256,068,849); value of slaves as above, one billion, two hundred and eighty million, one hundred and forty-five thousand, six hundred dollars ($1,280,145,600). Thus has the industry and political and domestic economy of the slaveholders, in two hundred and thirty years, been able to bring the value of their lands and themselves nearly up to the market value of their slaves; and all three together, lands, slaves, and slaveholders, to nearly half the value of the property of the Free States.

The valuation of the State of New York in 1855 was one billion, four hundred and one million, two hundred and eighty-five thousand, two hundred and seventy-nine dollars ($1,-401,285,279), being more than the whole value of the real estate of the Slave States in 1850, which, after deducting from the aggregate the value of the slaves in Louisiana, was one billion, three hundred and thirty-two million, six hundred and sixty-five thousand, four hundred and sixteen dollars ($1,332,665,-416). The value of the real and personal estate of Massachusetts in 1850 was more (slaves excepted) than that of the States of Virginia, North and South Carolina, Georgia, Florida, and Texas; the valuation of Massachusetts being five hundred and seventy-three million, three hundred and forty-two thousand, two hundred and eighty-six dollars ($573,342,286); that

8

of the six States mentioned being five hundred and seventy-three million, three hundred and thirty-two thousand, eight hundred and sixty dollars ($573,332,860.) In this calculation, South Carolina is reckoned at its State valuation of 1854. The whole area of Massachusetts is (Table IX.) four million, nine hundred and ninety-two thousand (4,992,000) acres; value of its whole property per acre, one hundred and fourteen dollars and eighty-five cents ($114.85.) The whole area of the six States above mentioned is (Table X.) three hundred and seventeen million, five hundred and seventy-six thousand, three hundred and twenty (317,576,320) acres; value of their whole property, except slaves, five hundred and seventy-three million, three hundred and thirty-two thousand, eight hundred and sixty dollars ($573,332,860), or one dollar and eighty-one cents ($1.81) per acre. Thus, Massachusetts is able to buy and pay for considerably more than half the great empire of slavery, and have more money left than the Pilgrims landed with at Plymouth; while Pennsylvania could easily buy out the other half.

Table XXXI. shows the number of miles of canals and railroads in operation in 1854, (with the cost of construction of such railroads), the number of miles of railroads in operation in January, 1855, and the amount of bank capital near January, 1855, in the several Free and Slave States. The first three columns of the tables are from the Census Compendium, the last two from the American Almanac for 1856.

Table XXXII. gives the total debt, amount of productive property, and the annual expenditure of the several Free and Slave States. The figures are from the American Almanac for 1856.

TABLE XXXI.

A Statement of the Number of Miles of Canals and Railroads in operation in 1854 (with the cost of construction), and the Miles of completed Railroads, and the Amount of Bank Capital, near January, 1855, in the several Free and Slave States.

FREE STATES.	Canals, miles. 1854.	Railroads, miles in operation. 1854.	Cost of Railroads. 1854.	Railroads, miles in operation. Jan'y, 1855.	Bank Capital 1854-5.
Connecticut	61	669	$20,857,357	625	$15,597,891
Illinois	100	1,262	25,420,000	1,964	2,513,790
Indiana	367	1,127	22,400,000	1,632	7,281,934
Iowa				54	
Maine	50	417	12,662,645	470	7,301,252
Massachusetts	100	1,283	55,602,687	1,437	54,492,660
Michigan		601	13,842,279	699	980,416
New Hampshire	11	512	11,185,254	502	3,626,000
New Jersey	147	408	11,533,505	444	5,314,885
New York	989	2,345	94,523,785	2,287	88,773,288
Ohio	921	2,367	44,927,058	2,423	7,166,581
Pennsylvania	986	1,464	58,494,675	1,690	19,864,825
Rhode Island		50	2,614,484	66	17,511,162
Vermont		422	14,116,195	556	3,275,656
Wisconsin		178	3,800,000	231	1,400,000
Total	3,682	13,105	$396,982,924	15,080	$230,100,340

SLAVE STATES.	Canals, miles. 1854.	Railroads, miles in operation. 1854.	Cost of Railroads. 1854.	Railroads, Miles in operation. Jan'y, 1855.	Bank Capital. 1854-5.
Alabama	51	221	$3,636,208	363	$2,296,400
Delaware	14	16	600,000	22	1,393,175
Florida		54	250,000	26	
Georgia	28	884	16,084,872	1,146	13,413,100
Kentucky	486	253	4,909,990	187	10,369,717
Louisiana	101	117	1,131,000	251	20,179,107
Maryland	184	597	26,024,620	545	10,411,874
Mississippi		155	3,070,000	67	240,165
Missouri	13	50	1,000,000	140	1,215,398
North Carolina	50	249	4,106,000	558	5,205,073
South Carolina		575	11,287,093	608	16,603,253
Tennessee		388	7,800,000	274	6,717,848
Texas				30	
Virginia	189	673	12,720,421	1,023	14,033,883
Total	1,116	4,212	$92,520,204	5,250	$102,078,948

TABLE XXXII.

Debt, Productive Property, and Annual Expenditure of the several Free and Slave States, compiled from State Returns, near January 1, 1855.

FREE STATES.	Total Debt of State. 1855.	Productive Property, exclusive of School Fund. 1855.	Ordinary Annual Expenditure, exclusive of Debts and Schools.	SLAVE STATES.	Total Debt of State. 1855.	Productive Property, exclusive of School Fund. 1855.	Ordinary Annual Expenditure, exclusive of Debts and Schools.
Maine	$685,500	$648,289	$150,000	Delaware	none.	$350,638	$11,000
New Hampshire	none.	none.	80,000	Maryland	$15,132,909	12,555,842	170,000
Vermont	"	"	100,000	Virginia	28,603,979	5,395,582	600,000
Massachusetts	6,739,555	8,967,509	600,000	North Carolina	3,409,633	600,000	75,000
Rhode Island	382,335	....	55,000	South Carolina	2,917,696	5,460,291	115,000
Connecticut	none.	406,000	120,000	Georgia	2,644,222	5,000,000	131,000
New York	26,047,898	38,800,000	750,000	Florida	none.	....	45,000
New Jersey	65,000	252,174	90,000	Alabama	6,168,887	700,000	100,000
Pennsylvania	40,613,160	35,060,667	425,000	Mississippi	7,271,707	....	130,000
Ohio	16,662,959	18,000,000	200,000	Louisiana	12,459,350	....	515,000
Michigan	3,213,245	....	125,000	Texas	12,436,991	....	100,000
Indiana	7,338,473	....	80,000	Arkansas	3,319,596	....	35,000
Illinois	13,994,615	....	125,000	Tennessee	8,744,857	2,244,827	165,000
Iowa	79,796	58,571	25,000	Kentucky	6,147,284	....	250,000
Wisconsin	100,000	....	40,000	Missouri	9,802,000	378,538	110,000
California	1,812,502	....	700,000		....	....	....
Total	$117,735,038	$102,193,210	$3,665,000	Total	$119,059,111	$32,685,718	$2,552,000

CHAPTER VIII.

EDUCATION. — I. COLLEGES.

THE first college established in the Free States was Harvard University, founded in 1636; which was sixteen years after the landing of the Pilgrims at Plymouth. The first college in the Slave States was that of William and Mary, in Virginia, founded in 1692, or eighty-four years after the settlement of Jamestown. The number of students in the former is now 365; in the latter, 82. The number of alumni of the former, 6,700; of the latter, 3,000. The number of volumes in the library of the former is 101,250; of the latter 5,000.

It will be seen by Tables **XXXIII** and **XXXIV**, taken from the American Almanac for 1856, and showing the present condition of the colleges in the two great sections, that the number of colleges is nearly the same in each. The comparative character and efficiency of these institutions, may be in some measure learned from the following facts. The number of volumes in the libraries of the Southern colleges is 308,011; in those of the northern, 667,297; over two to one. The number graduated at the South is 19,648; at the North 47,752; about two and one-half to one. The number of Ministers educated in the Southern colleges is 747, and in the Northern, 10,702; a ratio of fourteen to one.

It would indeed be interesting, were it possible, to compare these institutions in respect to value of buildings, apparatus, cabinets, &c.; but the statistics of these cannot be readily obtained. Still more difficult would it be to compare statistically the ability of professors and the standard of scholarship.

TABLE XXXIII.[*]

Colleges in the Slave States.

SLAVE STATES.	No. of Colleges.	No. of Instructors.	No. of Alumni.	No. of Ministers.	Students.	Volumes in Libraries.
Delaware	2	18	83	42	137	11,500
Maryland	5	69	607	13	399	33,292
Virginia	10	72	9,528	146	1,174	65,875
North Carolina ...	3	24	1,406	123	469	23,700
South Carolina ...	2	14	3,124	3	190	23,800
Georgia..........	5	34	1,359	133	643	25,700
Alabama..........	4	40	676	28	333	23,200
Mississippi	4	16	252	16	315	10,700
Louisiana	4	26	94	10	157	9,000
Tennessee	8	39	838	74	570	29,744
Kentucky	7	54	1,342	130	700[i]	27,900
Missouri	5	44	339	29	568	23,600
Total	59	450	19,648	747	5,655	308,011

TABLE XXXIV.

Colleges in the Free States.

FREE STATES.	No. of Colleges.	No. of Instructors.	No. of Alumni.	No. of Ministers.	Students.	Volumes in Libraries.
Maine...........	2	15	1,418	303	274	43,150
New Hampshire..	1	12	4,187	883	258	31,900
Vermont........	3	16	1,536	527	228	21,650
Massachusetts ...	4	47	9,404	2,612	807	122,750
Rhode Island....	1	10	1,860	500	225	34,000
Connecticut	3	43	7,407	1,956	669	91,000
New York.......	8	84	6,888	1,461	1,080	80,516
New Jersey......	3	54	3,855	837	449	28,000
Pennsylvania	9	66	8,298	741	959	71,180
Ohio	12	88	1,958	644	1,191	92,191
Indiana	4	27	546	158	300	19,600
Illinois	4	30	257	79	245	15,860
Michigan........	2	14	130		180	13,000
Wisconsin	5	11	8	1	30	2,500
Total	61	517	47,752	10,702	6,895	657,297

II. — PROFESSIONAL SCHOOLS.

The condition of the Professional Schools is shown by the following Table, taken from the same authority as the above. From this it appears that at the South a larger proportion of professional students are in the Law Schools than at the North. Next in order in this respect is Medicine, and last, Theology. Indeed, the Census Tables do not show where the great body of the Southern clergy are educated, since but 747 are returned from the colleges, and only 808 from the Theological Schools.

It will be noticed that the number of Professional Schools in the Slave States is 32, and in the Free States 65, or two to one. The ratio of Professors is a little larger. The number of Students in the former is 1,807, and in the latter 4,426. The number of volumes in the libraries of the former is 30,796, and in those of the latter, 175,951 ; more than five to one. The number graduated at the former, 3,812, and at the latter, 23,513 ; over six to one.

TABLE XXXV.

Showing the Condition of the Professional Schools in the North and the South, from the American Almanac for 1856.

SLAVE STATES.

Professional Schools.	Number of Schools.	Number of Professors.	Number of Students, 1854-5.	Number Educated.	Number of Vols. in Libraries.
Law	9	19	231	....	....
Medicine	13	75	1,307	3,004	....
Theology	10	28	269	808	30,796
Total	32	122	1,807	3,812	30,796

FREE STATES.

Professional Schools.	Number of Schools.	Number of Professors.	Number of Students, 1854–5.	Number Educated.	Number of Vols. in Libraries.
Law	9	19	240	....	....
Medicine	22	152	3,095	15,950	....
Theology	34	98	1,091	7,563	175,951
Total	65	269	4,426	23,513	175,951

III. — ACADEMIES, PRIVATE AND PUBLIC SCHOOLS.

In all the New England colonies, a law was passed in 1647, " That every township, after the Lord hath increased them to the number of fifty householders, shall appoint one to teach all children to write and read ; and when any town shall increase to the number of one hundred families, they shall set up a grammar school ; the masters thereof being able to instruct youth so far as they may be fitted for the university." See Colonial Laws.

Again, in Connecticut we find the following : " Forasmuch as the good Education of Children is of singular behoofe and benefit to any Commonwealth, and whereas, many parents and masters are too indulgent and negligent of theire duty in that kinde : —

" It is therefore ordered by this Courte and Authority thereof that the Selectmen of every Town, in the Several precincts and quarters where they dwell, shall have a vigilant eye over theire brethren and neighbours to see first that none of them shall suffer so much Barbarism in any of theire families as not to endeavour to teach by themselves or others theire Children and apprentices so much Learning as may enable them per- fectly to read the Inglish tounge, and knowledge of the Capi- tall Laws, upon penalty of twenty shillings for each neglect therein." See " Code of Laws established by the General

Court of Conn., May, 1650," as recorded in Vol. II. of the Colonial Records of Conn.

In the year 1671, or twenty-four years after the establishment of public schools by law in the Plymouth Colonies, and over thirty years after Harvard college was founded, and a printing press set up in Cambridge, Gov. Berkley, at that time Governor of Virginia, said of that State: "I thank God there are no free schools nor printing, and I hope we shall not have these hundred years, for learning has brought disobedience and heresy and sects into the world, and printing has divulged them, and libels against the best government; God keep us from both."

The following Tables Nos. XXXVI., XXXVII., XXXVIII., and XXXIX., show the condition of the Academies, Private and Public Schools in 1850, as given in the Census Compendium:

TABLE XXXVI.

Academies and Private Schools in the Slave States.

SLAVE STATES.	Number.	Teachers.	Pupils.	Annual Income.	Scholars in Colleges, Academies and Public Schools.
Alabama	166	380	8,290	$164,165	37,237
Arkansas	90	126	2,407	27,937	11,050
Delaware	65	94	2,011	47,832	11,125
Florida ....,...	34	49	1,251	13,089	3,129
Georgia	219	318	9,059	108,983	43,299
Kentucky	330	600	12,712	252,617	85,914
Louisiana	143	354	5,328	193,077	31,003
Maryland	223	503	10,787	232,341	45,025
Mississippi	171	297	6,628	73,717	26,236
Missouri	204	368	8,829	143,171	61,592
North Carolina	272	403	7,822	187,648	112,430
South Carolina	202	333	7,467	205,489	26,035
Tennessee..........	264	404	9,928	155,902	115,750
Texas	97	137	3,389	39,384	11,500
Virginia	317	547	9,068	234,372	77,774
Total	2,797	4,913	104,976	$2,079,724	699,079

TABLE XXXVII.

Academies and Private Schools in the Free States.

FREE STATES.	Number.	Teachers.	Pupils.	Annual Income.	Scholars in Colleges, Academies and Public Schools.
California	6	5	170	$14,270	219
Connecticut	202	329	6,996	145,967	79,003
Illinois	83	160	4,244	40,488	130,411
Indiana	131	233	6,185	63,520	168,754
Iowa	33	46	1,111	7,980	30,767
Maine..............	131	232	6,648	51,187	199,745
Massachusetts	403	521	13,436	310,177	190,924
Michigan	37	71	1,619	24,947	112,382
New Hampshire.....	107	183	5,321	43,202	81,237
New Jersey.........	225	453	9,844	227,588	88,244
New York	887	3,136	49,328	810,332	727,222
Ohio	206	474	15,052	149,392	502,826
Pennsylvania	524	914	23,751	467,843	440,977
Rhode Island.......	46	75	1,601	32,748	25,014
Vermont............	118	257	6,864	48,935	100,785
Wisconsin..........	58	86	2,723	18,796	61,615
Total..............	3,197	7,175	154,893	$2,457,372	2,940,125

TABLE XXXVIII.

Public Schools of the Slave States.

SLAVE STATES.	Number.	Teachers.	Pupils.	Annual Income of Public Schools.
Alabama	1,152	1,195	28,380	$315,602
Arkansas	353	355	8,493	43,763
Delaware	194	214	8,970	43,861
Florida	69	73	1,878	22,386
Georgia	1,251	1,265	32,705	182,231
Kentucky	2,234	2,306	71,429	211,852
Louisiana	664	822	25,046	349,679
Maryland	898	986	33,111	218,836
Mississippi	782	826	18,746	254,159
Missouri	1,570	1,620	51,754	160,770
North Carolina	2,657	2,730	104,095	158,564
South Carolina	724	739	17,838	200,600
Tennessee	2,680	2,819	104,117	198,518
Texas	349	360	7,946	44,088
Virginia....................	2,930	2,997	67,353	314,625
Total......................	18,507	19,307	581,861	$2,719,534

TABLE XXXIX.

Public Schools of the Free States.

FREE STATES.	Number.	Teachers.	Pupils.	Annual Income of Public Schools.
California....................	2	2	49	$3,600
Connecticut.................	1,656	1,787	71,269	231,220
Illinois......................	4,052	4,248	125,725	349,712
Indiana.....................	4,822	4,860	161,500	316,955
Iowa........................	740	828	29,556	51,492
Maine.......................	4,042	5,540	192,815	315,436
Massachusetts	3,679	4,443	176,475	1,006,795
Michigan	2,714	3,231	110,455	167,806
New Hampshire	2,381	3,013	75,643	166,944
New Jersey	1,473	1,574	77,930	216,672
New York	11,580	13,965	675,221	1,472,657
Ohio	11,661	12,886	484,153	743,074
Pennsylvania................	9,061	10,024	413,706	1,348,249
Rhode Island...............	416	518	23,130	100,481
Vermont....................	2,731	4,173	93,457	176,111
Wisconsin	1,423	1,529	58,817	113,133
Total......................	62,433	72,621	2,769,901	$6,780,337

It will be seen that in the South a larger proportion of the children who attend School, attend at private Schools, than at the North. Still the number of scholars in these Schools is but a slight fraction over two-thirds as great at the South as at the North, and the amount of money paid for the support of these Schools nearly $400,000 less in the slave than in the free States.

It is to be regretted that we are unable to compare these Schools in other respects, but figures can carry us no further at this time. Perhaps by comparing the different sections of this chapter we may be able to form a just opinion.

It will be observed that the Public School statistics would not be materially affected for purposes of comparison, were those of the private Schools added to them.

The number of public Schools at the South is 18,507 ; at the North, 62,433 ; a ratio of about three and one-half to one. Teachers at the South, 19,307 ; at the North, 72,621 ; almost four to one. The number of Scholars at the South is 581,861, and at the North, 2,769,901; nearly five to one, and over 2,000,000 more at the North than at the South. Indeed, if we compare the *entire* number attending all Schools (Colleges Academies, private and public Schools,) we find in the North a majority over the South of 2,241,046, which is now more than three times the entire number attending School in the Southern States. In other words, more than four-fifths of the children attending School in the Union are in the free States. The amount of money expended annually for these Schools is, in the Slave States, $4,799,258; and in the free States, $9,237,709.

The State of Ohio is not quite two-thirds as large as Virginia. Virginia has 77,764 scholars at School and Ohio has 502,826.

The area of Kentucky is very nearly equal to that of Ohio, the population almost exactly one-half as great, and the number of scholars at School a little more than one-sixth.

Massachusetts is one-fourth as large as South Carolina, and contains nearly four times as many white inhabitants. The number of scholars attending School in South Carolina, is 26,025; in Massachusetts, 190,924.

The amount expended for Schools, both public and private, in South Carolina, is $406,089; in Massachusetts, it is $1,316,972; a difference of almost a million of dollars.

The whole number of scholars at School in the fifteen slave-holding States, is 699,079; in the single State of New York, it is 727,222.

Such are the figures of the Census for 1850.

Great effort has been made to obtain such statistics as to show the condition of all grades of Schools at the *present time*, much more fully than it can be learned from the census for the time when that was taken. Not enough, however, could be obtained for purposes of just comparison, the annual reports from the Slave States being so exceedingly meagre. So far, however, as such reports could be obtained, they show that the difference between the free and slave States, in regard to education, is constantly increasing.

This arises from the want of any regular system for education of the poorer classes, who are increasing so rapidly in the Southern States. Proofs of this might be given, were it not a well known fact.

On page 146 of the Census Compendium, it is said of "Georgia — no public Schools strictly, but Schools receive a certain amount of aid from State funds. This is true for many Southern States."

The State of South Carolina appropriates annually the sum of $75,000 to free Schools. Gov. Manning, in his message of Nov. 28, 1853, says that "under the present mode of applying it, that liberality is really the profusion of the prodigal, rather than the judicious generosity which confers real benefit."

In the State of Arkansas, only forty Schools were reported to the Commissioner for 1854. It is of course utterly impossible to obtain any reliable information with regard to the Schools there, though we may form a very just opinion concerning their character in such a community. The Commissioner says, "The great obstacle to the organization of common Schools is not so much a deficiency in the means to sustain them, as it is the indifference that pervades the public mind on the subject of education."

The amount expended by the State of Virginia, in 1854, for the education of poor children, was $69,404. For the maintenance of the public guard, $73,189.

New England, whose area is less than one-twelfth greater, appropriated $2,000,000 for Public Schools, and felt secure without a public guard.

The State of South Carolina has established one Free State Scholarship; the State of Massachusetts has established forty-eight.

In Kentucky, the average number of scholars at school in 1854, was 76,429. In Ohio it was 279,635. The total amount of money distributed (for public schools) during the year 1854, in Kentucky, was $146,047. The amount appropriated by the State of Ohio for the same purpose, was $2,266,609 ; a difference of over $2,000,000.

There are very many items of expenditure for educational purposes at the North, for which the corresponding sums at the South cannot be ascertained. Among these are Teachers' Institutes, holden annually in every county in many of the Northern States ; Teachers' Associations, Normal Schools, School-houses, &c. The value of school buildings in the State of Ohio in 1854, was $2,197,384, and in Massachusetts it was, in 1848, $2,750,000 ; even in the little State of Rhode Island it is $319,293. The amount raised by taxation for educational purposes is now, in each of the three states, New York, Pennsylvania, and Massachusetts, over one million dollars annually.

The Report of the Commissioner of Public Schools to the Mayor and City Council of Baltimore, for the year 1851, gives the following facts :

The value of school buildings in the city of Baltimore, is $105,729 ; New York, $552,457 ; Philadelphia, $858,224 ; and in Boston $729,502.*

The following table is copied from the same report :

TABLE XL.

Showing the Condition of Public Schools in certain Cities.

CITIES.	Population.	Schools	Teach-ers.	Pupils.	Cost of Tuition.
Boston	138,788	203	353	21,678	$237,000
New York	517,000	207	332	40,055	274,794
Philadelphia	409,000	270	781	·48,056	341,888
Baltimore	169,012	36	138	8,011	32,423
Cincinnati	·116,000	17	124	6,006	81,623
St. Louis	81,000	73	168	6,642	....

* Besides this there were paid for new buildings in Boston, $56,000; in Philadelphia, $24,473 ; and in Cincinnati, $10,000.

The population of Baltimore is 30,000 greater than that of Boston. Baltimore has 8,000 scholars at school, for whose instruction she pays $30,000. Boston has 20,000, and pays for instruction, $230,000.

It would indeed be interesting, were it a matter capable of statistical comparisons, to trace the results of the superior educational advantages enjoyed by the children of the North; to compare the philosophers, orators, and statesmen, men of skill, science, or literature, authors, poets, and sculptors, of the two sections. To see how many of those who are most distinguished at the South were born, bred, and educated at the North.

DeBow, in a labored article in the Census Compendium, in behalf of the southern schools, says: "An examination of Massachusetts shows, out of 2,357 'students,' mentioned, 711, or one-third nearly, born out of the State, and 152, or one-fifteenth, born in the South. On the other hand a southern town, taken at random, furnished one out of three editors, four out of twelve teachers, two out of seven clergymen, born in the non-slaveholding States."

The presumption is that *not so large* a proportion of the students in Southern institutions are sent there from the North to be educated, and that, on the other hand, not so large a proportion of the editors, teachers and clergymen of the North are of Southern birth and education.

IV. — LIBRARIES.

The following tables, Nos. XLI. and XLII., are of great importance in connection with the subject of education, as showing the literary tastes, habits of thought, and sources of enjoyment, of the people. These tables also show the character of the various institutions in the two sections, more correctly than it could be ascertained from almost any other source, embracing as they do the Public School, Sunday School, College and Church libraries:

TABLE XLI.

Libraries other than Private in the Slave States.

SLAVE STATES.	Public		School.		Sunday School.		College.		Church		Total.	
	Number.	Volumes.	Number.	Volumes.	Number.	Volumes.	Number.	Volumes.	Number.	Volumes.	Number.	Volumes.
Alabama	4	3,848	32	3,500	15	5,775	5	7,500	...	...	56	20,623
Arkansas	1	250	...	...	2	170	...	...	...	...	3	420
Delaware	4	10,250	...	...	12	2,700	1	5,000	...	...	17	17,950
Florida	1	1,000	2	800	4	860	...	...	...	...	7	2,660
Georgia	3	6,500	11	1,800	15	1,988	9	21,500	4	1,200	38	31,788
Kentucky	47	40,424	...	...	18	4,617	11	33,225	...	...	80	79,466
Louisiana	5	9,800	2	12,000	...	...	3	5,000	5	1,850	10	26,800
Maryland	17	54,750	8	6,335	84	28,315	10	33,792	...	...	124	125,042
Mississippi	4	7,264	103	3,650	6	730	4	10,093	1	600	117	21,737
Missouri	13	23,106	13	17,150	66	14,500	4	19,700	9	1,647	97	75,056
North Carolina	4	2,500	1	1,500	19	2,352	5	21,593	...	...	38	29,592
South Carolina	16	73,758	3	2,750	...	...	7	30,964	...	...	26	107,472
Tennessee	9	5,373	2	5,100	18	2,498	5	9,925	...	...	34	22,896
Texas	3	2,100	3	430	5	1,600	1	100	...	...	12	4,230
Virginia	21	32,595	6	2,706	11	1,975	14	50,856	2	330	54	88,462
Total	152	273,518	186	57,721	275	63,463	79	249,248	21	5,627	695	649,577

TABLE XLII.

Libraries other than Private in the Free States.

FREE STATES.	Public. Number.	Public. Volumes.	School. Number.	School. Volumes.	Sunday School. Number.	Sunday School. Volumes.	College. Number.	College. Volumes.	Church. Number.	Church. Volumes.	Total. Number.	Total. Volumes.
California												
Connecticut	42	38,609	4	5,039	107	38,445	8	82,600	3	265	164	165,318
Illinois	33	35,982	29	5,875	86	12,829	4	7,800			152	62,486
Indiana	58	46,238	3	1,800	85	11,265	4	8,700	1	400	151	68,403
Iowa	4	2,650	4	160	24	2,980					32	5,790
Maine	77	51,439	11	2,225	131	26,988	8	39,625	9	1,692	236	121,969
Massachusetts	177	257,737	792	104,645	433	165,476	18	141,400	42	14,757	1,462	684,015
Michigan	280	65,116	119	31,427	15	3,500	3	7,900			417	107,943
New Hampshire	47	42,017	3	1,200	70	20,117	3	19,975	6	2,450	129	85,759
New Jersey	77	43,903	10	4,080	35	8,564	4	24,000	2	338	128	80,885
New York	43	197,229	10,802	1,388,729	137	33,294	25	138,870	6	2,698	11,013	1,760,820
Ohio	65	65,703	13	9,665	248	53,910	22	56,573	4	975	352	186,826
Pennsylvania	90	184,666	30	17,161	226	58,071	21	77,050	26	26,452	393	363,400
Rhode Island	26	42,007	12	5,814	50	23,765	1	31,000	7	1,756	96	104,342
Vermont	30	21,061	16	9,700	38	10,020	9	23,280	3	580	96	64,641
Wisconsin	9	12,040	33	2,163	28	5,017	2	1,800			72	21,020
Total	1,058	1,106,397	11,881	1,589,683	1,713	478,858	132	660,573	109	52,723	14,911	3,888,234

9*

From these it will be seen that the total number of volumes in the libraries of the South, is 649,577; in those of the North, 3,888,234; a difference more than 3,000,000 in favor of the free States. Six volumes in the libraries of the North to one at the South. But we need not compare aggregates when the difference is so overwhelming. The Sunday School libraries of the North are nearly twice as great as the College libraries of the South; and the College libraries of the North greater than *all* the libraries of the South.

Maine has more volumes in her libraries than South Carolina, Rhode Island than Virginia, or even more than all the five states, Georgia, Alabama, Mississippi, Louisiana, and Florida; and Massachusetts more than all the fifteen slave States.

Michigan and Arkansas are very nearly equal, both in age and territory, Michigan having been admitted into the Union in 1837, and Arkansas in 1836; while the area of Michigan is 56,243 square miles, and that of Arkansas 52,198. Michigan has 107,943 volumes in her libraries, Arkansas has 420; a ratio of 257 to 1.

The public school libraries alone of the single state of New York, contain more than twice as many volumes as all the libraries together of the whole South. Nor are we to suppose that because *Common School* Libraries, they are necessarily inferior either in cost or character. We learn from the American Almanac for the present year, that in the State of Illinois " 690 school libraries, of 321 volumes each, were distributed throughout ⊥he state. The aggregate cost of these 221,490 volumes was $147,222, or an average of $213 for each library."

If the New York common school libraries were purchased at a similar cost, (over sixty-six cents per volume,) their *value* is doubtless greater than that of all the libraries in the fifteen slave States.

V. — ILLITERATE.

Thus far the large figures have been all in one direction, but here the case is different. The South is in advance and still advancing.

The following tables, Nos XLIII. and XLIV., show the number unable to read and write. It will be seen that the number of native white citizens of this class in the free States is 248,725, and in the slave States 493,026, a number about twice as great in a population of far less than half.

The number of native white adults who cannot read and write, in the State of Tennessee, is 77,017, in a white population of 756,836. The number in New York, 23,241, in a white population of 3,048,325.

TABLE XLIII.

Persons in the Slave States over Twenty Years of Age who cannot Read and Write.

SLAVE STATES.	Whites.	Free Colored.	Natives.	Foreign.	Native Whit_s.
Alabama	33,757	235	33,853	139	33,618
Arkansas	16,819	116	16,908	27	16,792
Delaware	4,536	5,645	9,777	404	4,132
Florida...............	3,859	270	3,834	295	3,564
Georgia	41,200	467	41,261	406	40,794
Kentucky.............	66,687	3,019	67,359	2,347	64,340
Louisiana	21,221	3,389	18,339	6,271	14,950
Maryland	20,815	21,062	38,426	3,451	17,364
Mississippi...........	13,405	123	13,447	81	13,324
Missouri	36,281	497	34,917	1,861	34,420
North Carolina........	73,566	6,857	80,083	340	73,226
South Carolina........	15,684	880	16,460	104	15,580
Tennessee	77,522	1,097	78,114	505	77,017
Texas................	10,525	58	8,095	2,488	8,037
Virginia	77,005	11,515	87,383	1,137	75,868
Total	512,882	55,230	548,256	19,856	493,026

The number in Georgia is 40,794, in a white population of 521,572, and of Pennsylvania it is 41,944, in a white population of 2,258,160.

Again. The number of white inhabitants over twenty years of age, in the state of New Hampshire, is 174,232. The number of native white adults who cannot read and write, is 893, or 1 in 201. In Connecticut it is 1 in 277; in Vermont 1 in 284; and in Massachusetts 1 in 517. In South Carolina, on the other hand, it is 1 in 7; in Virginia 1 in 5, and in North Carolina 1 in 3.

Such facts as these show the condition and character of the schools in the North and the South more clearly than all other statistics combined.

TABLE XLIV.

Persons in the Free States over Twenty Years of Age who cannot Read and Write.

FREE STATES.	Whites.	Free Colored.	Natives.	Foreign.	Native Whites.
California	5,118	117	2,318	2,917	2,201
Connecticut.......:...	4,739	567	1,293	4,013	826
Illinois..............	40,054	1,229	35,336	5,947	34,107
Indiana..............	70,540	2,170	69,445	3,265	67,275
Iowa	8,120	33	7,076	1,077	7,043
Maine...............	6,147	135	2,134	4,148	1,999
Massachusetts	27,539	806	1,861	26,484	1,055
Michigan............	7,912	369	5,272	3,009	4,903
New Hampshire.......	2,957	52	945	2,064	893
New Jersey...........	14,248	4,417	12,787	5,878	8,370
New York............:	91,293	7,429	30,670	68,052	23,241
Ohio	61,030	4,990	56,958	9,062	51,968
Pennsylvania.........	66,928	9,344	51,288	24,989	41,944
Rhode Island	3,340	267	1,248	2,359	981
Vermont	6,189	51	616	5,624	565
Wisconsin............	6,361	92	1,551	4,902	1,459
Total	422,515	32,068	280,793	173,790	248,725

CHAPTER IX.

In the language of DeBow : " In every country the press must be regarded a great educational agency. Freedom of speech and of the press are the inalienable birthright of every American citizen, and constitute the ægis of his liberties."

The earliest newspaper in North America was the Boston News-Letter, issued April 24, 1704. There were in 1775 but 37 Newspapers in the American Colonies.*

Of these there were three in South Carolina, two in each of the States Maryland, Virginia, and North Carolina, and one in Georgia; making in all 10 in the present slaveholding States. In New Hampshire there was one, two in Rhode Island, four in Connecticut, the same number in New York, seven in Massachusetts, and nine in Pennsylvania ; making 27 in the present non-slaveholding States. At that time the white population in the two sections was very nearly equal.

The following tables show the number of papers and their circulation, in the several States, in 1810; also the number of papers in 1828, and of papers and periodicals in 1840. They also show the character of the newspaper and periodical press, the number of copies printed annually, the number of papers, and the circulation of each class, in 1850.

---

* It will be perceived by looking on the 54th page of the Census Compendium, that there is a descrepancy between the several numbers and the amount given. I presume the separate numbers to be correct.

TABLE XLV.

Newspapers and Periodicals in the Slave States in 1810, 1828 and 1840.

SLAVE STATES.	1810.		1828,	1840
	Papers.	Circulation.	Papers.	Papers and Periodicals.
Alabama	....	....	10	28
Arkansas	....	....	2	9
Delaware..................	2	166,400	4	8
Florida....................	....	....	2	10
Georgia	13	707,200	18	40
Kentucky	17	618,800	23	46
Louisiana.................	11	763,900	9	37
Maryland	21	1,903,200	37	49
Mississippi	4	83,200	6	31
Missouri	....	....	5	35
North Carolina............	10	416,000	20	29
South Carolina............	10	842,400	16	21
Tennessee	6	171,600	8	56
Texas.....................	....	....	....	....
Virginia..................	23	1,289,600	34	56
Total.....................	117	6,962,300	194	455

TABLE XLVI.

Newspapers and Periodicals in the Free States in 1810, 1828, and 1840.

FREE STATES.	1810.		1828.	1840.
	Papers.	Circulation.	Papers.	Papers and Periodicals.
California.................	....	....	....	....
Connecticut	11	657,800	33	44
Illinois....................	....	....	4	52
Indiana	1	15,600	17	76
Iowa......................	....	....	....	4
Maine.....................	....	....	29	41
Massachusetts	32	2,873,000	78	105
Michigan	....	....	2	33
New Hampshire	12	624,000	17	33
New Jersey	8	332,800	22	40
New York.................	66	4,139,200	161	302
Ohio	14	473,200	66	143
Pennsylvania..............	71	4,542,200	185	229
Rhode Island..............	7	332,800	14	18
Vermont	14	682,400	21	33
Wisconsin.................	....	....	....	6
Total	236	14,673,000	649	1,159

TABLE XLVII.

Newspapers and Periodicals Published in the Slave States, 1850.

SLAVE STATES.	Daily.		Tri-Weekly.		Semi-Weekly.		Weekly.	
	Number.	Number of copies printed annually.	Number.	Number of copies printed annually.	Number.	Number of copies printed annually.	Number.	Number of copies printed annually.
Alabama.........	6	869,201	5	266,500	....	....	48	1,509,040
Arkansas	....	....	....	....	3	....	9	377,000
Delaware........	....		....		....	62,400	7	358,800
Florida..........	....	.:....	1	31,200	....		9	288,600
Georgia	5	1,086,110	3	146,380	:....		37	2,609,776
Kentucky.......	9	2,243,584	7	1,125,280	....	....	38	3,053,024
Louisiana	11	9,947,140	6	676,000	....	....	37	1,646,684
Maryland.......	6	15,806,500	4	499,700	....	....	54	3,166,124
Mississippi......	....		4	245,440	....	....	46	1,507,064
Missouri........	5	3,380,400	4	273,000	....	....	45	2,406,560
North Carolina..	....		5	414,310	....	....	40	1,530,204
South Carolina..	7	5,070,600	5	549,250	....	....	27	1,413,880
Tennessee.......	8	4,407,666	2	266,240	....	....	36	2,139,644
Texas...........	....		5	525,400	....	....	29	771,524
Virginia	15	4,992,850	12	1,416,550	....	....	55	2,518,568
Total...........	72	47,803,551	63	6,435,250	3	62,400	517	25,296,492

TABLE XLVIII.

Newspapers and Periodicals Published in the Free States, 1850.

FREE STATES.	Daily.		Tri-Weekly.		Semi-Weekly.		Weekly.	
	Number.	Number of copies printed annually.	Number.	Number of copies printed annually.	Number	Number of copies printed annually.	Number.	Number of copies printed annually.
California.......	4	626,000	....		....	....	3	135,200
Connecticut.....	7	1,752 800	4	374,400	....	....	30	2,117,232
Illinois	8	1,120,540	4	214,500	....	....	84	3,575,936
Indiana.........	9	1,153,092	2	195,000	....	....	95	2,920,736
Iowa	....		2	577,200	....	....	25	923,000
Maine	4	964,040	5	302,900	....	....	39	2,906,124
Massachusetts...	22	40,498,444	4	351,000	11	2,070,016	126	20,371,104
Michigan	3	1,252,000	2	52,000	....	3,116,360	47	1,685,736
N. Hampshire...	....		....		....		35	3,538,152
New Jersey	6	2,175,350	....		....		43	1,900,288
New York.......	51	63,928,685	8	776,100	13	....	308	39,205,920
Ohio............	26	14,285,633	10	1,047,930	....	62,400	201	13,334,204
Pennsylvania ...	24	50,416,788	2	78,000	1	25,200	261	27,359,384
Rhode Island....	5	1,768.450	....	.:.....	2	228,800	12	963,300
Vermont	2	172.150	....		1	....	30	2,142,712
Wisconsin	6	1,053,245	4	198,250	....	....	35	1,395,992
Total...........	177	181.167,217	47	4,167,280	28	5,502,776	1,374	124,475,020

TABLE XLIX.

Newspapers and Periodicals published in the Slave States in 1850.

SLAVE STATES.	Semi-Monthly.		Monthly.		Quarterly.		Aggregate.*	
	Number.	Number of copies printed annually.	Number.	Number of copies printed annually.	Number.	Number of copies printed annually.	Number.	Number of copies printed annually.
Alabama	1	18,000	....	....	....	....	60	2,662,741
Arkansas	....	....	....	....	....	....	9	377,000
Delaware	....	....	....	....	....	....	10	421,200
Florida	....	....	....	....	....	....	10	319,800
Georgia..............	6	228,600	....	....	....	....	51	4,070,866
Kentucky............	8	160,950	....	....	....	....	62	6,582,838
Louisiana............	....	....	1	146,400	....	....	55	12,416,224
Maryland............	1	48,000	3	92,400	....	....	68	19,612,724
Mississippi	....	....	....	....	....	....	50	1,752,504
Missouri	....	....	7	135,600	....	....	61	6,195,560
North Carolina......	6	76,050	....	....	....	....	51	2,020,564
South Carolina.......	5	102,600	....	....	2	9,600	46	7,145,930
Tennessee	....	....	4	127,200	....	....	50	6,940,750
Texas	....	....	....	....	....	....	34	1,296,924
Virginia	3	267,600	1	24,000	1	4,000	87	9,223,068
Total	30	901,800	16	525,600	3	13,600	704	81,038,693

* This aggregate is the aggregate of this table together with the last.

TABLE L.

Newspapers and Periodicals published in the Free States in 1850.

FREE STATES.	Semi-Monthly.		Monthly.		Quarterly.		Aggregate.*	
	Number.	Number of copies printed annually.	Number.	Number of copies printed annually.	Number.	Number of copies printed annually.	Number.	Number of copies printed annually.
California.........	....	....	....	....	....	....	7	761,200
Connecticut......	....	....	1	'6,000	2	8,800	46	4,267,932
Illinois	3	43,200	7	147,900	1	900	107	5,102,276
Indiana..........	1	48,000	....	....	....	....	107	4,316,828
Iowa.............	....	....	2	12,600	....	....	29	1,512,800
Maine	....	....	1	30,000	....	....	49	4,203,064
Massachusetts ...	3	61,800	29	1,357,200	7	24,000	202	64,820,564
Michigan	3	134,400	3	123,600	....	....	58	3,247,736
New Hampshire ..	1	15,600	2	13,800	....	....	38	3,067,552
New Jersey	2	23,040	....	....	....	....	51	4,098,678
New York........	9	1,704,000	36	6,629,808	3	24,600	428	115,385,473
Ohio	23	1,781,640	....	....	1	24,000	261	30,473,407
Pennsylvania	19	6,972,000	....	....	2	7,600	309	84,898,672
Rhode Island.....	....	....	....	....	....	....	19	2,756,950
Vermont	....	....	2	24,000	....	....	35	2,567,662
Wisconsin	....	....	1	18,000	....	....	46	2,665,487
Total............	64	10,783,680	84	8,362,208	16	89,900	1,790	334,146,281

* This aggregate is the aggregate of this table together with the last.

TABLE LI.

Character of the Newspaper and Periodical Press.—Number of copies printed annually in the Slave States, as given in 1850.

SLAVE STATES.	Literary and Miscellaneous.	Neutral and Independent.	Political.	Religious.	Scientific.
Alabama	265,200	313,000	1,889,169	158,400	36,972
Arkansas	171,600	....	205,400	....	....
Delaware	46,800	....	374,400	....	....
Florida	....	....	202,800	117,000	....
Georgia	1,411,976	747,340	1,491,350	239,200	181,000
Kentucky	650,800	250,400	5,245,888	429,450	6,300
Louisiana	657,300	3,335,100	8,356,224	52,000	15,600
Maryland	14,654,000	8,400	4,196,924	669,400	84,000
Mississippi	233,480	....	1,519,024	....	....
Missouri	608,800	....	5,496,280	90,480	....
North Carolina	266,200	113,750	1,457,664	182,950	....
South Carolina	474,800	2,140,400	4,310,930	1,092,040	24,800
Tennessee	206,200	503,930	5,138,580	195,500	....
Texas	350,324	148,400	660,400	137,800	....
Virginia	247,880	1,251,900	6,698,176	1,001,112	24,000
Total	20,245,360	8,812,620	47,243,209	4,364,832	372,672

TABLE LII.

Character of the Newspaper and Periodical Press.—Number of copies printed annually in the Free States, as given in 1850.

FREE STATES.	Literary and Miscellaneous.	Neutral and Independent.	Political.	Religious.	Scientific.
California	135,200	626,000	....	....	....
Connecticut	489,900	....	3,422,432	223,200	7,200
Illinois	721,700	403,770	3,384,162	499,044	93,600
Indiana	647,504	....	3,569,324	100,000	....
Iowa	36,000	187,200	1,281,800	7,800	....
Maine	987,216	....	2,501,680	438,568	275,600
Massachusetts	11,794,304	13,591,000	32,996,800	4,405,200	2,033,260
Michigan	456,500	26,000	2,556,836	134,400	74,000
New Hampshire	579,480	....	1,673,672	778,000	36,400
New Jersey	181,640	93,900	3,823,138	....	....
New York	18,449,016	37,317,010	45,463,015	12,438,432	1,718,000
Ohio	3,865,880	4,220,805	18,865,282	3,334,240	187,200
Pennsylvania	18,515,028	21,908,548	37,808,960	6,588,136	78,000
Rhode Island	280,800	782,500	1,693,650	....	....
Vermont	208,600	....	2,025,430	333,632	....
Wisconsin	130,000	....	2,517,487	....	18,000
Total	57,478,768	79,156,733	163,583,668	29,280,652	4,521,260

TABLE LIII.

Number of Papers, and the Circulation of each Class, in the Slave States, in 1850.

SLAVE STATES.	Literary and Miscellaneous. Number.	Literary and Miscellaneous. Circulation.	Neutral and Independent. Number.	Neutral and Independent. Circulation.	Political. Number.	Political. Circulation.	Religious. Number.	Religious. Circulation.	Scientific. Number.	Scientific. Circulation.	Aggregate. Number.	Aggregate. Circulation.
Alabama	11	5,100	1	1,000	45	24,336	2	3,450	1	711	60	34,597
Arkansas	3	3,300	.	.	6	3,950	.	.	.	.	9	7,250
Delaware	2	900	.	.	8	6,600	.	.	.	.	10	7,500
Florida	.	.	.	.	7	3,500	3	2,250	.	.	10	5,750
Georgia	18	29,638	6	3,046	20	20,900	3	4,600	4	9,300	51	67,484
Kentucky	12	14,900	2	800	42	55,936	5	12,525	1	525	62	84,686
Louisiana	13	22,025	6	12,000	34	45,522	1	1,000	1	300	55	80,847
Maryland	20	71,000	1	700	39	31,637	6	13,950	2	7,000	68	124,287
Mississippi	10	4,490	.	.	40	26,380	.	.	.	.	50	30,870
Missouri	17	19,400	.	.	42	48,340	2	2,740	.	.	61	70,480
North Carolina	8	5,675	2	875	35	24,564	6	5,725	.	.	51	36,839
South Carolina	10	12,700	5	8,300	24	28,115	5	4,600	2	2,000	46	55,715
Tennessee	5	10,350	2	1,610	36	33,147	7	22,770	.	.	50	67,877
Texas	17	6,737	1	1,400	14	8,350	2	2,650	.	.	34	19,137
Virginia	10	5,690	5	4,200	62	51,988	9	25,256	1	2,000	87	89,134
Total	156	211,905	31	33,931	454	413,265	51	101,516	12	21,836	704	782,453

TABLE LIV.

Number of Papers, and the Circulation of each Class, in the Free States, in 1850.

FREE STATES	Literary and Miscellaneous		Neutral and Independent		Political		Religious		Scientific		Aggregate	
	Number.	Circulation.	Number.	Circulation.	Number.	Circulation.	Number.	Circulation.	Number.	Circulation.	Number.	Circulation.
California	3	2,600	4	2,000	....	....	....	....	....	....	7	4,600
Connecticut ..	12	11,200	....	....	28	34,916	4	5,400	1	1,200	45	52,716
Illinois	22	17,725	1	1,290	73	51,111	8	12,097	3	6,400	107	88,623
Indiana	21	12,452	....	....	84	47,900	2	3,000	....	....	107	63,352
Iowa	2	1,000	1	1,200	25	20,150	1	650	....	....	29	23,000
Maine	15	20,458	....	....	29	29,695	4	8,434	1	5,300	49	63,887
Massachusetts	80	283,027	9	50,700	82	171,387	24	117,650	14	94,205	209	716,969
Michigan	13	13,625	1	200	39	28,793	8	5,600	2	4,500	58	52,718
New Hampshire	10	11,790	....	....	22	32,186	5	15,500	1	700	38	60,176
New Jersey	6	4,010	1	300	44	40,144	....	....	....	....	51	44,454
New York	101	528,908	15	127,370	263	399,755	37	507,246	12	59,500	428	1,622,779
Ohio	37	111,790	6	13,485	192	189,304	21	90,130	5	10,400	261	415,109
Pennsylvania .	71	445,364	12	70,396	198	267,940	28	198,018	1	1,500	310	983,218
Rhode Island .	6	5,400	1	2,500	12	18,075	....	....	....	....	19	25,975
Vermont	5	5,550	....	....	27	33,990	3	6,416	....	....	35	45,956
Wisconsin	3	2,500	....	....	42	29,236	....	....	1	1,500	46	33,236
Total	407	1,477,399	51	269,441	1,160	1,394,582	140	970,141	41	185,205	1,799	4,296,768

It will be seen on examination of these Tables, that in 1810 the number of papers in the Slave States was 117, and in the free States, 236 ; almost exactly two to one. The ratio of circulation was a little larger.

In 1828, the number of papers at the North was to that at the South as 3 to 1 ; and in 1840 as 2 1-2 to 1. The circulation for those years is not given.

In 1850, the number of papers at the South was 704; at the North 1,799; while the circulation at the South was 782,453, and at the North, 4,296,768 ; or over five at the North to one at the South.

The circulation in Michigan, is 52,000 ; in Arkansas, 7,000 ; in Kentucky, 84,000 ; in Ohio, 415,000 ; in South Carolina, 55,000 ; in New Hampshire, 60,000 ; in Mississippi, 30,000 ; and in New Jersey, 44,000 ; in Maryland, 124,000, (which is far the largest circulation of any Southern State) ; and in Massachusetts, 716,969. The circulation in Massachusetts, is but little less than that in all the slave States ; that in Pennsylvania is greater by one-fourth than of that entire section ; while the circulation of New York is considerably more than double that of the whole dominion of slavery. The circulation of the single paper, the New York Weekly Tribune, is at the present time greater than was, in 1850, the circulation of all the newspapers in the States Virginia, North Carolina, and Mississippi ; indeed, we might add a couple more slave States, and it would still be greater.

On examining the character of the Newspapers and Periodicals in the two sections, we see that a large proportion (more than one-half,) of the Southern Papers, are political; and a much larger proportion than of the Northern, the proportion in the North being less than one-third. In this class they have a circulation nearly equal to one-third of the Northern, while of the literary and miscellaneous, neutral and independent, it is one-seventh ; in the scientific, one-eighth ; and in the religious, one-ninth.

These ratios are in some instances greater, if we compare the number of copies printed annually.

The number of copies, of neutral and independent papers, printed in a year, in the slave States, is 8,000,000 ; and in the free States, 79,000,000. Of the religious, in the slave States, 4,000,000; and in the free States, 29,000,000. Of the scientific, the number is, at the South, 372,000; and at the North, 4,000,000 ; while of the political, the number at the South, is 47,000,000; and at the North, 163,000,000.

The number of copies of scientific papers printed in the fifteen Southern States, is 372,000. The number printed in Massachusetts alone, is 2,000,000 ; more than five times as many as in all the slave States. The number of copies of religious papers printed in the fifteen slave States, is 4,000,000 ; in the State of New York, 12,000,000. Of neutral and independent papers there are, in the slave States, 8,000,000 ; and in Pennsylvania, 21,000,000.

The political press of either Massachusetts or Pennsylvania, issues annually more copies than half the political presses of the slave States ; while that of New York issues but a slight fraction less than the whole.

Finally. The daily press of the South issues 47,000,000 annually; that of Massachusetts and Pennsylvania the same ; and of the free States, 181,000,000. The weekly press of the South issues 25,000,000 copies; that of Pennsylvania 27,000,-000; of New York, 39,000,000; and of the free States, 124,000,000. The New York Daily Herald had a circulation nearly, if not quite, half as great as all the daily papers of the slave States, in 1850.

The aggregate number of copies printed annually in Arkansas, is 377,000 ; in Wisconsin, 2,665,000. In Kentucky, 6,000,000 ; in Ohio, 30,000,000. In Maryland, Virginia, North Carolina, South Carolina, Georgia, Alabama, Missis-

10*

sippi, Florida, Louisiana, and Texas, together less than Massachusetts.

In the fifteen slave states, 81,000,000; in Pennsylvania,
84,000,000; in New York, 115,000,000; and in the sixteen
free states, 334,000,000.

CHAPTER X.

POST OFFICE DEPARTMENT.

The following tables, Nos. LV., LVI., and LVII., will show the amounts actually credited for the transportation of the mails in the several States, and the amount of postages collected in the same, for the fiscal years ending June 30, 1850, and June 30, 1855.

Few tables can be more suggestive, or more amply repay a careful investigation, than these.

At the present day, the energy and business character of a people, their roads, railroads, steamboats, and other means of transportation, are all given, in a word, in their Post-Office reports.

TABLE LV.

Showing the Amounts actually credited for the Transportation of Mails, and the Amounts of Postage collected in the Slave and Free States in 1850.

SLAVE STATES.	Total Postage Collected.	Transporta- tion.	FREE STATES	Total Postage Collected.	Transporta- tion.
Alabama	$75,937 75	$143,798 70	California	$227,152 82	$111,515 87
Arkansas	17,215 53	61,244 90	Connecticut...	119,971 81	62,176 13
Delaware	12,521 38	6,489 87	Illinois	115,184 53	156,685 71
Florida	13,793 24	31,701 55	Indiana.......	83,638 03	76,225 82
Georgia	101,749 42	146,772 94	Iowa	26,568 86	24,850 05
Kentucky	86,472 49	87,121 70	Maine	89,761 92	46,690 25
Louisiana	116,936 06	68,464 61	Massachusetts.	358,120 72	132,164 84
Maryland.....	121,864 61	143,150 97	Michigan	62,387 69	39,634 58
Mississippi....	55,536 01	84,256 58	N. Hampshire.	59,902 20	27,662 00
Missouri	83,787 95	101,313 23	New Jersey....	66,156 20	42,813 37
N. Carolina...	46,647 07	154,977 40	New York.....	933,977 13	324,970 14
S. Carolina....	76,108 62	108,488 80	Ohio..........	286,311 24	138,836 32
Tennessee	64,185 86	74,142 59	Pennsylvania .	396,699 91	146,105 64
Texas	28,474 12	114,744 83	Rhode Island..	39,328 34	12,088,20
Virginia	141,579 13	169,687 83	Vermont	58,965 44	50,643 93
....	....	....	Wisconsin	60,725 35	34,759 77
Total	$1,042,809 24	$1,496,356 50	Total	$2,975,852 19	$1,427,822 63

TABLE LVI.

Showing the Amounts actually credited for the Transportation of the Mails, and the Amount of Postage collected in the Slave States in 1855.

SLAVE STATES.	Letter Postage.	Newspaper Postage.	Stamps Sold.	Total Postage Collected.	Transportation.
Alabama..........	$46,416	$13,583	$44,514	$104,514	$226,816
Arkansas	16,894	4,828	8,941	30,664	117,659
Delaware	9,967	2,377	7,298	19,644	9,243
Florida	8,167	2,343	8,764	19,275	77,558
Georgia	59,117	16,066	73,880	149,063	216,003
Kentucky.........	59,307	15,065	55,694	130,067	144,161
Louisiana........	69,140	13,833	50,778	133,753	133,810
Maryland.........	82,029	31,712	77,743	191,485	192,743
Mississippi.......	36,092	11,464	31,182	78,739	170,785
Missouri..........	71,372	14,537	53,742	139,652	185,096
North Carolina....	26,831	11,692	34,235	72,759	148,249
South Carolina....	36,156	8,075	47,368	91,600	192,216
Tennessee	42,070	13,238	48,377	103,686	116,091
Texas.............	37,373	8,532	24,530	70,436	209,936
Virginia	92,562	28,499	96,799	217,861	245,592
Total	$693,493	$195,844	$66,845	$1,553,198	$2,385,953

TABLE LVII.

Showing the Amounts actually credited for the Transportation of the Mails, and the Amount of Postage collected in the Free States in 1855.

FREE STATES.	Letter Postage.	Newspaper Postage	Stamps Sold.	Total Postage Collected.	Transportation.
California	$141,833	$11,319	$81,437	$234,591	$135,386
Connecticut.......	75,691	24,254	79,284	179,230	81,462
Illinois	142,177	32,457	105,252	279,887	280,038
Indiana...........	95,248	24,578	60,578	180,405	190,480
Iowa	44,540	9,680	28,198	82,420	84,428
Maine	75,779	15,413	60,165	151,358	82,218
Massachusetts	239,894	33,226	259,062	532,184	153,091
Michigan	77,223	15,201	49,763	142,188	148,204
New Hampshire...	46,225	10,995	38,387	95,609	46,631
New Jersey	66,645	11,556	31,495	109,697	80,084
New York	734,453	106,206	542,498	1,383,157	481,410
Ohio	237,457	47,227	167,958	452,643	421,870
Pennsylvania	301,646	64,073	217,293	583,013	251,833
Rhode Island......	23,812	4,520	30,291	58,624	13,891
Vermont	44,465	12,036	36,314	92,816	64,437
Wisconsin	65,406	13,959	33,538	112,903	92,842
Total	$2,412,494	$436,700	$1,719,513	$4,670,725	$2,608,295

A few of the facts which stand forth prominent in these Tables, are the following :

In 1850, only two slave States, Delaware and Louisiana, paid for the transportation of their mails by the amount of postages collected.

Of the free states, Illinois alone did not.

In the slave States, the postages for that year less than paid for the transportation, by nearly half a million of dollars. In the free States, the postages more than paid for the transportation, by over a million and a half of dollars.

In 1855, this difference is very greatly increased.

The postages of the slave States less than paid the cost of transportaion by over $800,000, while the free State postages more than paid the transportation, by over $2,000,000.

In the slave territory, the only State which paid for transportation of its mails, by its postages, was Delaware. In the free States, the only States which did not, were Illinois, Indiana, Iowa, and Michigan.

Neither North Carolina, South Carolina, Mississippi, Alabama, or Texas, paid half the expense of transporting their mails, by postages received; while Florida paid less than a fourth, and Arkansas less than a fifth.

Massachusetts paid for her own transportation, and had a surplus remaining of more than four times the amount of postage collected in South Carolina.

New Hampshire, Connecticut, and Pennsylvania, each paid for their transportation, by their postages, more than twice over, and Rhode Island more than four fold.

The postages of New York are not an eighth less than those of all the slave States, while the expense of transportation is but little more than one-fifth the expense in those States.

The fifteen slave States did not pay, by postages, two-thirds the expense of transporting their mails.

The free States paid for theirs, and had a surplus of over

$2,000,000; half a million more than all the postages collected in the slave States.

In other words, the free States, in this matter, support themselves, pay the deficit in the slave States and have over $1,200,000 besides.

CHAPTER XI.

THE following tables, Nos. LVIII. and LIX. show the
amount contributed in the several States, for the Missionary,
Tract, and Bible cause, by all the principal Christian denominations, except the Methodist. This denomination is not
included in the tables, from the fact that all receipts are returned by conferences, which are frequently made up of several
parts of States, thus precluding the possibility of separating so

TABLE LVIII.

*Showing the Amount contributed in the Slave States for purposes of Christian
Benevolence in 1855, together with the Value of Churches in 1850.*

SLAVE STATES.	Amount con-tributed for the Bible cause.	Amount con-tributed for Missionary purposes.	Amount con-tributed for the Tract cause.	Value of Churches, 1850.
Alabama	$3,351	$5,963	$477	$1,244,741
Arkansas	2,950	455	110	149,686
Delaware	1,037	1,003	163	340,345
Florida	1,957	340	5	192,600
Georgia	4,532	9,846	1,468	1,327,112
Kentucky	5,956	6,953	1,366	2,295,353
Louisiana	1,810	334	1,099	1,940,495
Maryland	8,909	20,677	5,365	3,974,116
Mississippi	1,067	4,957	267	832,622
Missouri	4,711	2,712	936	1,730,135
North Carolina	6,197	6,010	1,419	907,785
South Carolina	3,984	15,248	3,222	2,181,476
Tennessee	8,383	4,971	1,807	1,246,951
Texas	3,985	349	127	408,944
Virginia	9,296	22,106	6,894	2,902,220
Total...............	$68,125	$101,934	$24,725	$21,674,581

TABLE LIX.

Showing the Amount contributed in the Free States for purposes of Christian Benevolence in 1855, together with the Value of Churches in 1850.

FREE STATES.	Amount contributed for the Bible cause.	Amount contributed for Missionary purposes.	Amount contributed for the Tract cause.	Value of Churches. 1850.
California............	$1,900	$192	$5	$288,400
Connecticut..........	24,528	48,044	15,872	3,599,330
Illinois..............	28,403	10,040	3,786	1,532,305
Indiana	6,755	4,705	1,491	1,568,906
Iowa	4,216	1,750	2,005	235,412
Maine*	5,449	13,929	....	1,794,209
Massachusetts*	43,444	128,505	....	10,504,888
Michigan	5,554	4,935	1,114	793,180
New Hampshire*	6,271	11,963	....	1,433,266
New Jersey	15,475	19,946	3,546	3,712,863
New York...........	123,386	172,115	61,233	21,539,561
Ohio	25,758	19,890	9,576	5,860,059
Pennsylvania.........	25,360	43,412	12,121	11,853,291
Rhode Island	2,669	9,440	2,121	1,293,600
Vermont*	5,709	11,094	....	1,251,655
Wisconsin	4,790	2,216	474	512,552
Total	$319,667	$502,174	$131,972	$67,773,477

* $18,628 as given in the Report for the four together.

as to give the amount from each State. Indeed, there is some difficulty in dividing the amount justly between the slave and free States; but this is not as great as in dividing it between all the several States, since the sum collected in all the conferences, made up partly of slave and partly of free Territory, is but $35,000, which could make but little difference in the result, however it might be divided. The amount collected for the Tract cause and the support of missions, was, for the past year, in the Northern conferences, $225,000, of which $35,000 was from conferences embracing both slave and free territory. According to the Annals of Southern Methodism, for the year 1855, the amount raised in the Methodist Church South, in the year 1854, was $168,931, "and for the year just closing, the amount will fall somewhat below that," says the author.

Taking these facts and dividing the $35,000 according to the best of our information, the amount contributed for these purposes, in the Methodist Church, is a few thousand dollars greater in the free than in the slave States. This of course is exclusive of the operations of the "Book Concern," &c., &c.

The amount contributed by all other denominations is given by States in the tables, which are compiled from the last annual report of the several societies.

The amount contributed in the slave States, for the Bible cause, was, during the past year, $68,125; in the free States, $319,667; a ratio of over 4 1-2 to 1. The amount contributed for the support of missions was, in the slave States, $101,934, and in the free States, $502,174; almost exactly five dollars to one. The amount contributed in the slave States for the publication and distribution of Tracts, was $24,725; and in the free States, $131,972; a ratio still greater, and over five dollars at the North to one at the South. The amount contributed in the State of Massachusetts, for the support of missions, is greater than in all the slave States, while the amount contributed in the State of New York, both for the missionary and Bible cause, was nearly twice as great as in all the territory of slavery.

It will be seen that the value of Churches in the slave States is $21,674,581, and in the free States, $67,773,477; a ratio of more than 3 to 1 — the Churches of New York being equal in value to those of the fifteen slave States.

The amount contributed in the several States for the various benevolent objects which from time to time present themselves, it is impossible to ascertain. But the report of the Portsmouth Relief Association, just published, shows the amount received from the different States "For the relief of Portsmouth, Va., during the prevalence of the yellow fever in that town in 1855." It is certainly gratifying to see that the call for help was so promptly answered from the most distant States. The amount of money contributed by the slave States, exclusive of

11

Virginia, in which State the sickness prevailed, was $12,182. In the free States it was $42,547, or 3 and 1-2 times as much in the free as in the slave States. Including the State of Virginia, the amount given by the slave States was $33,398, or $9,141 more given by the sixteen free States than by the fifteen slave States. This is exclusive of provisions and other valuable supplies, amounting to thousands of dollars, sent from all parts of the Union.

CHAPTER XII.

MASSACHUSETTS AND SOUTH CAROLINA.

In this chapter are given the full statistics of Massachusetts and South Carolina, in 1850, by counties, as published in Compendium of the Census; to which are added tables showing the number of men furnished by the several States in the Revolutionary war, the number of pensioners in 1840, and extracts showing the action and condition of the State of South Carolina in the war of the Revolution.

TABLE LX.

Statistics of Massachusetts — Census of 1850.

COUNTIES.	POPULATION.							
	Whites.			Colored.	All Classes.		Total Population.	
	Male.	Female	Total.		Male.	Female.	1850.	1840.
Barnstable	17,803	17,350	35,153	123	17,868	17,408	35,276	32,548
Berkshire	23,958	24,300	48,258	1,333	24,629	24,962	49,591	41,745
Bristol	36,641	38,018	74,659	1,533	37,342	38,850	76,192	60,164
Dukes	2,306	2,181	4,487	53	2,328	2,212	4,540	3,958
Essex	63,862	66,820	130,682	618	64,148	67,152	131,300	94,987
Franklin	15,407	15,372	30,779	91	15,455	15,415	30,870	28,812
Hampden	24,943	25,837	50,780	503	25,171	26,112	51,288	37,366
Hampshire......	17,392	18,011	35,403	329	17,550	18,182	35,732	30,897
Middlesex.......	76,918	83,758	160,676	707	77,286	84,097	161,383	106,611
Nantucket	4,119	3,939	8,058	394	4,391	4,061	8,452	9,012
Norfolk.........	38,562	40,081	78,643	249	38,679	40,213	78,892	53,140
Plymouth	27,720	27,521	55,241	456	27,948	27,749	55,697	47,373
Suffolk	68,622	73,857	142,479	2,038	69,557	74,960	144,517	95,773
Worcester	65,840	64,312	130,152	637	66,165	64,624	130,789	95,313

TABLE LX.—*Continued.*

COUNTIES.	NATIVITIES, DWELLINGS, &c.				EDUCATION AND RELIGION.								
	Born out of State.		Dwellings.	Families.	Colleges, Academies, and Private Schools.		Public Schools.		Total Educational Income.	White Scholars during the year.	Whites 5 and under 20 years old.	Whites over 20 unable to read and write.	Accommodation of Churches—Persons.
	United States.	Foreign Countries.			Pupils.	Annual Income.	Pupils.	Annual Income.					
Barnstable	496	953	6,582	7,255	1,082	$10,435	7,682	$24,876	$35,311	10,049	12,014	59	26,802
Berkshire	10,583	5,819	8,638	9,460	881	26,028	7,523	23,795	49,823	10,513	15,699	949	40,705
Bristol	9,278	10,401	12,134	15,240	1,118	7,750	13,378	73,540	81,290	16,818	23,898	2,718	55,765
Dukes	302	89	771	908	...	...	897	2,636	2,636	1,104	1,361	7	3,820
Essex	18,440	16,684	18,878	26,945	2,634	54,658	25,158	122,923	177,581	29,582	40,633	2,320	92,489
Franklin	3,088	1,397	5,832	6,230	269	8,310	7,360	21,963	25,273	8,734	9,909	237	24,850
Hampden	10,406	8,034	9,083	9,750	560	7,783	8,666	39,986	47,769	11,916	15,723	1,311	36,065
Hampshire	3,839	3,286	5,905	6,694	791	27,721	7,677	26,660	54,381	9,205	11,533	391	30,935
Middlesex	32,252	31,122	23,450	30,241	1,978	97,246	26,728	183,390	280,636	34,525	48,906	5,338	105,891
Nantucket	766	465	1,285	1,670	356	8,836	1,232	9,278	13,114	1,792	2,446	74	5,021
Norfolk	8,946	15,650	12,545	15,690	1,350	23,070	14,086	87,149	110,219	16,922	23,460	3,101	51,125
Plymouth	2,935	3,243	9,506	11,557	468	10,692	10,781	50,170	60,862	13,722	17,342	439	43,075
Suffolk	23,162	49,632	16,567	25,416	1,800	33,000	17,230	248,356	381,356	24,304	40,945	7,443	78,025
Worcester	18,193	17,249	21,709	25,619	1,192	12,549	28,077	92,073	104,622	31,595	40,056	3,172	98,260

TABLE LX.—*Continued.*

COUNTIES.	LAND OCCUPIED OR IMPROVED.				LIVE STOCK UPON FARMS.				AGRICULTURAL PRODUCTS.			
	Farms.	Acres Improved.	Acres Unimproved.	Value with Improvements and Implements.	Horses, Asses, and Mules.	Neat Cattle.	Sheep.	Swine.	Wheat, Bushels.	Rye and Oats, Bushels.	Indian Corn, Bushels.	Irish and Sweet Potatoes, Bushels.
Barnstable........	789	27,786	40,556	$1,278,828	934	3,836	1,566	1,283	546	22,561	52,639	34,756
Berkshire........	2,897	272,489	174,956	9,577,926	5,310	32,608	79,333	7,587	7,802	386,655	240,899	359,642
Bristol..........	2,647	105,522	98,140	7,101,582	2,646	13,090	5,711	6,451	189	73,505	164,064	250,488
Dukes...........	265	21,926	11,794	686,620	233	1,739	9,643	750	45	5,608	12,895	9,899
Essex	2,708	145,921	54,204	9,582,992	2,768	17,828	2,108	6,761	1,435	59,261	158,264	339,423
Franklin........	2,587	197,232	93,753	6,833,281	3,372	23,464	23,829	4,731	3,948	145,450	223,359	185,114
Hampden........	2,615	193,153	96,843	7,420,723	3,709	21,755	14,973	6,408	3,076	215,986	252,213	305,637
Hampshire......	2,955	211,219	86,983	7,554,456	3,986	22,748	32,835	6,725	4,867	177,595	272,870	292,734
Middlesex.......	4,298	220,208	128,111	19,417,796	5,237	30,980	1,844	10,765	1,098	125,997	269,908	586,804
Nantucket.......	58	8,792	4,265	149,605	89	597	977	153	55	1,278	8,206	5,997
Norfolk.........	2,637	107,884	67,444	13,748,505	3,811	12,656	580	8,209	356	32,362	112,132	253,158
Plymouth.......	2,447	101,185	114,254	6,048,442	2,458	11,855	5,384	4,574	251	43,952	105,243	208,402
Suffolk.........	76	3,642	190	671,245	96	470	2	218	.....	1,383	2,691	10,069
Worcester.......	7,245	516,682	251,083	22,713,930	8,201	66,373	9,865	16,509	7,543	354,584	476,107	738,261

11*

TABLE LX.—Continued.

AGRICULTURAL PRODUCTS.

COUNTIES.	Peas and Beans, Bushels.	Barley, Bushels.	Buckwheat, Bushels.	Butter and Cheese, Pounds.	Hay, Tons.	Hops, Pounds.	Clover & other Grass Seeds, Bushels.	Flaxseed, Bushels.	Flax, Pounds.	Maple Sugar, Pounds.	Molasses, Gallons.	Tobacco, Pounds.
Barnstable	2,529	2,714	63	118,083	9,142		24					
Berkshire	4,127	12,746	43,347	3,635,952	92,460	1,121	486	53	520	316,288	958	
Bristol	2,492	4,130	313	420,812	28,552		2,072					
Dukes	35	774		27,677	2,015							
Essex	5,212	12,222	463	717,346	57,968	63	268	11	420			
Franklin	1,485	8,189	5,485	1,218,685	52,766	18,090	207	7	190	268,607	2,392	14,590
Hampden	3,350	1,082	20,649	1,226,756	48,749	172	738	1	15	52,626	91	68,156
Hampshire	1,419	5,782	11,287	1,334,541	59,064	1,743	139		17	152,777	911	55,200
Middlesex	9,646	9,735	3,836	1,033,588	81,992	65,636	686					
Nantucket	47	928		21,271	1,489	5						
Norfolk	3,952	5,462	454	437,249	41,588	81	381					
Plymouth	871	3,267	239	505,294	28,582	12	152					
Suffolk	297	505		1,680	2,446		6			5,227	841	
Worcester	8,247	44,849	9,759	4,466,068	145,094	39,672	928					

TABLE IX.—*Concluded.*

COUNTIES	MANUFACTURES — Produced in Families	Establishments — Annual Product	Establishments — Hands Employed	Establishments — Capital	AGRICULTURAL PRODUCTS — Wine, Gallons	Value of Orchard Produce	Value of Produce of Market Gardens	Value of Animals Slaughtered	Beeswax and Honey, Pounds	Silk Cocoons, Pounds	Wool, Pounds
Barnstable	$3,682	$817,031	765	$587,890	51	$8,241	$5,087	$52,322	....	....	4,124
Berkshire	8,557	4,267,706	3,872	3,177,795	....	10,604	4,966	208,635	17,761	....	256,289
Bristol	6,990	12,595,695	9,536	6,854,615	15	18,678	27,263	193,201	8,722	....	14,390
Dukes	853	305,070	88	56,700	....	1,286	....	16,470	....	....	22,430
Essex	14,580	22,906,805	35,267	12,895,647	251	65,727	182,431	174,468	2,114	....	5,956
Franklin	56,929	1,662,584	1,949	896,752	....	23,696	740	164,676	7,662	7	78,690
Hampden	11,482	6,653,548	7,836	6,655,590	547	13,137	16,994	180,242	5,283	....	41,529
Hampshire	26,697	3,410,745	3,453	2,004,748	10	19,094	2,631	205,845	5,961	....	108,540
Middlesex	17,908	26,548,932	29,356	20,473,880	2,623	134,640	220,982	310,917	3,529	....	5,475
Nantucket	....	1,077,448	166	617,900	....	160	2,994	5,492	80	....	2,970
Norfolk	25,702	13,223,596	15,628	5,433,300	91	55,458	186,796	229,809	1,047	....	879
Plymouth	953	6,713,906	8,024	2,397,305	21	19,205	13,502	176,102	3,352	....	18,643
Suffolk	....	32,018,869	25,296	10,887,690	20	2,473	10,020	4,856	136	....	9
Worcester	31,000	18,940,211	24,762	10,518,330	1,059	91,596	25,664	577,889	8,911	....	80,212

TABLE LXI.
Statistics of South Carolina — Census of 1850.

COUNTIES	Whites Male	Whites Female	Whites Total	Colored Free	Colored Slave	All Classes Male	All Classes Female	Total Population 1850	Total Population 1840	Born out of State United States	Born out of State Foreign Countries	Dwellings	Families
Abbeville	6,884	6,815	12,699	357	19,262	15,968	16,350	32,318	29,351	540	261	2,391	2,391
Anderson	6,782	7,085	13,867	94	7,514	10,422	11,053	21,475	18,493	763	79	2,440	2,445
Barnwell	6,201	6,088	12,289	311	14,008	13,322	13,286	26,608	21,471	60	64	2,460	2,460
Beaufort	3,012	2,985	5,947	579	32,279	18,946	19,859	38,805	35,794	190	122	1,385	1,385
Charleston	12,925	12,283	25,208	3,861	54,775	40,158	43,686	83,844	82,661	1,880	5,954	5,350	5,541
Chester	3,997	4,006	8,003	148	9,887	8,940	9,098	18,038	17,747	332	216	1,541	1,641
Chesterfield	3,817	3,861	6,678	218	3,894	5,380	5,410	10,790	8,574	734	85	1,263	1,263
Colleton	3,470	3,305	6,775	819	21,872	13,877	14,559	28,466	25,548	40	55	1,318	1,878
Darlington	3,531	3,216	6,747	42	10,041	8,524	8,806	16,830	14,822	351	28	1,313	1,818
Edgefield	8,121	8,131	16,252	285	22,725	19,617	19,645	39,262	32,852	720	216	3,019	3,027
Fairfield	3,679	3,389	7,068	90	14,246	10,792	10,612	21,404	20,165	210	235	1,282	1,283
Georgetown	1,158	1,035	2,198	201	18,258	9,998	10,649	20,647	18,274	130	21	575	575
Greenville	6,648	6,722	13,370	95	6,491	9,934	10,222	20,156	17,839	838	108	2,351	2,351
Horry	2,807	2,715	5,522	49	2,075	3,880	3,766	7,646	5,755	405	9	980	980
Kershaw	2,321	2,360	4,681	214	9,578	7,225	7,248	14,473	12,281	196	82	928	928
Lancaster	2,888	2,969	5,857	117	5,014	5,463	5,525	10,988	9,907	67	85	1,096	1,096
Laurens	5,563	5,807	11,370	84	11,953	11,615	11,792	23,407	21,584	191	82	2,132	2,182
Lexington	3,658	3,692	7,350	23	5,557	6,395	6,535	12,930	12,111	68	69	1,812	1,812
Marion	4,962	4,962	9,781	106	7,520	8,474	8,933	17,407	13,982	180	6	1,856	1,868
Marlborough	2,504	2,529	5,033	156	5,600	5,351	5,438	10,789	8,408	562	89	929	929
Newberry	3,630	3,612	7,242	213	12,688	10,013	10,130	20,143	18,350	93	54	1,513	1,494
Orangeburgh	4,080	4,040	8,120	78	15,384	11,607	11,975	23,582	18,519	81	85	1,515	1,515
Pickens	6,495	6,610	13,106	120	3,679	8,383	8,571	16,904	14,856	1,116	52	2,332	2,833
Richland	3,541	3,223	6,764	501	12,978	10,205	10,038	20,243	16,397	644	468	1,588	1,618
Spartanburgh	9,118	9,193	18,311	50	8,089	13,160	13,240	26,400	23,669	331	39	3,185	3,185
Sumter	4,888	4,990	9,813	342	23,065	16,395	16,825	33,220	27,892	854	74	1,908	1,908
Union	4,630	4,687	9,317	143	10,892	9,759	10,098	19,852	18,936	387	60	1,734	1,734
Williamsburgh	1,982	1,920	3,902	37	8,508	6,158	6,289	12,447	10,327	100	15	717	717
York	5,593	5,706	11,299	127	8,007	9,723	9,710	19,433	18,383	1,187	150	2,190	2,190

TABLE LXI.—Continued.

COUNTIES.	Colleges, Academies, and Private Schools — Pupils	Colleges, Academies, and Private Schools — Annual Income	Public Schools — Pupils	Public Schools — Annual Income	Total Educational Income	White Scholars during year	Whites 5 and under 20 years old	Whites over 20 unable to read and write	Accommodation of Churches — persons	Farms	Acres Improved	Acres Unimproved	Value with Improvements and Implements	Horses, Asses, and Mules	Neat Cattle
Abbeville	599	$18,105	1,179	$16,245	$34,350	2,917	5,075	109	27,500	1,814	212,628	425,081	$5,006,610	8,918	25,959
Anderson	395	8,746	826	6,480	15,226	2,550	5,629	979	22,885	1,986	178,455	282,495	2,559,483	5,796	19,215
Barnwell			450	5,160	5,160	1,530	4,965	701	19,450	1,558	197,676	957,893	2,877,754	6,528	34,678
Beaufort	302	9,320	598	1,800	11,120	1,270	2,301	206	18,640	842	231,289	687,469	5,601,350	5,026	48,388
Charleston	3,082	139,875	1,196	19,549	159,424	4,342	8,578	184	40,770	682	183,235	626,495	5,903,220	5,023	41,903
Chester	130	1,588	413	4,512	6,100	1,248	3,033	214	8,250	844	192,801	143,138	3,171,782	5,139	13,586
Chesterfield	36	1,500	355	4,540	6,040	789	2,653	1,181	8,975	548	52,511	241,317	903,477	1,890	9,508
Colleton	230	7,696	64	760	8,456	930	2,714	727	10,920	888	121,475	632,458	3,627,534	4,221	43,312
Darlington	46	1,380	620	7,320	8,700	854	2,740	267	9,000	857	123,162	540,408	2,935,880	3,980	13,717
Edgefield	283	11,484	1,093	18,398	29,882	2,453	6,546	533	26,400	2,030	263,379	688,042	5,654,033	10,255	38,001
Fairfield	417	16,650		13,200	29,850	1,059	2,663	154	10,075	675	121,593	289,563	3,289,563	4,678	13,797
Georgetown	281	7,000	170	1,800	8,800	455	772	12	9,900	550	49,609	237,268	5,704,920	1,403	12,908
Greenville	150	6,000	960	9,800	15,800	1,960	5,501	1,821	15,100	1,068	131,727	318,514	2,102,038	4,312	14,047
Horry			170	1,675	1,675	473	2,294	189	8,250	731	33,664	239,730	885,840	907	14,814
Kershaw	75	2,672	488	5,800	8,472	417	1,859	98	9,050	383	61,102	472,971	1,443,868	2,674	11,690
Lancaster			340	3,520	3,520	905	2,375	305	10,860	580	100,728	296,960	1,568,576	2,945	10,895
Laurens	225	3,066	569	8,630	11,696	1,438	4,500	426	28,000	1,603	182,525	196,937	4,060,899	7,286	22,948
Lexington	98	2,160	863	8,400	10,560	971	2,923	633	10,800	887	70,730	282,957	1,075,318	3,353	14,609
Marion	50	2,000	700	3,700	5,700	1,331	4,034	774	11,050	1,374	124,306	437,841	2,680,544	3,642	22,617
Marlborough			350	6,634	6,634	923	1,990	748	9,850	621	85,395	652,342	1,987,613	2,483	8,750
Newberry			524	14,172	14,172	1,148	2,777		16,825	1,045	182,952	204,505	3,703,458	5,942	18,952
Orangeburgh			1,181	8,833	8,833	982	3,293	575	16,449	1,206	169,703	782,681	3,176,806	4,931	26,815
Pickens			1,120	2,883	2,883	2,051	5,415	2,161	23,970	1,231	181,333	474,756	1,708,635	4,134	16,046
Richland	895	54,650	370	1,600	56,250	874	2,336	83	9,270	543	93,206	235,695	2,075,052	2,991	11,575
Spartanburgh	175	7,200	185	11,500	18,700	1,353	7,532	85	26,550	1,555	89,426	354,281	2,792,626	7,353	23,840
Sumter	304	7,660	1,000	9,311	16,971	1,364	3,811	942	24,250	1,343	207,666	651,935	3,749,065	6,154	18,949
Union	159	3,402	504	4,817	8,219	1,689	3,593	876	14,490	869	226,274	235,333	3,161,665	5,364	13,277
Williamsburgh			474	3,150	3,150	570	1,530	279	5,100	454	162,787	432,440	861,538	1,974	18,387
York	260	2,125	378	1,411	3,536	1,447	4,316	509	7,830	1,252	133,596	283,924	2,798,890	5,352	15,153

TABLE LXI.—*Continued.*

AGRICULTURAL PRODUCTS.

Counties	Sheep	Swine	Wheat, Bushels.	Rye and Oats, Bushels.	Indian Corn, Bushels.	Irish and Sweet Potatoes, Bushels.	Peas and Beans, Bushels.	Barley, Bushels.	Buckwheat, Bushels.	Butter and Cheese, Pounds.	Hay, Tons.	Hops, Pounds.	Clover & other Grass Seeds, Bushels.	Flaxseed, Bushels.	Flax, Pounds.	Maple Sugar, Pounds.	Cane Sugar, Hhds. of 1000 Pounds.
Abbeville	16,364	66,548	99,101	282,278	1,054,233	130,843	15,014	1,173		269,646	6,509	6		10	100		
Anderson	18,135	43,242	120,382	209,695	820,549	146,061	25,414	173	20	240,277	2,326					200	21
Barnwell	13,106	68,303	10,886	15,583	839,629	169,869	98,088			26,425	5	2					20
Beaufort	16,892	37,855	2,465	29,913	492,671	485,219	76,353			88,421	17	5					
Charleston	13,415	30,247	235	40,664	417,627	669,350	77,813		25	83,101	2,440						
Chester	7,514	29,579	55,864	74,476	573,070	43,342	3,743	50	200	128,420	483						33
Chesterfield	4,628	21,167	12,954	41,706	257,651	59,484	21,588			48,210	2,286		376				
Colleton	15,150	37,062	2,443	34,671	382,044	241,269	69,819			120,198	59						
Darlington	6,191	36,650	12,092	73,955	471,357	119,458	92,135			37,114							
Edgefield	18,588	73,742	62,810	287,088	1,155,489	180,115	60,558	281		226,325	13						2
Fairfield	7,123	23,080	30,233	48,914	529,461	72,546	9,587	60		115,940	387	3					
Georgetown	4,336	9,311	245	21,891	136,312	209,800	7,210		25	12,845							1
Greenville	9,255	36,555	60,682	111,074	687,784	88,516	19,863	15		116,903	22						
Horry	10,298	29,830	494	481	127,100	55,205	8,155			21,755	563				186		
Kershaw	6,182	21,024	6,621	23,982	362,165	40,605	25,688			36,170	66			5	15		
Lancaster	6,630	20,997	21,644	66,337	352,218	62,042	13,403			90,828	163			39			
Laurens	11,583	55,288	129,694	193,721	895,291	112,004	11,428	1,315		165,286	2						
Lexington	5,961	25,182	2,986	34,530	382,518	153,657	19,625			41,834	234			1	20		
Marion	11,442	46,620	11,088	26,281	476,718	96,586	43,842			50,888	6				12		
Marlborough	4,419	22,260	79,515	59,922	351,670	85,690	27,219	1,081		39,016							
Newberry	8,888	38,033	13,465	100,494	664,058	195,320	24,643		13	105,075	8						
Orangeburgh	12,797	41,680	42,052	8,225	614,418	113,077	76,611			172,893	47						
Pickens	6,124	37,786	6,538	127,821	694,011	92,880	14,760	5		50,841	460		30				
Richland	4,603	19,163	102,993	84,688	433,998	876,815	49,098			211,055	2,469	10					
Spartanburgh	14,026	51,921	7,410	154,509	873,654	49,354	16,654			65,897	55						
Sumter	13,931	50,742	68,286	45,354	750,520	143,314	87,984	231		135,012	575						
Union	7,360	31,262	1,472	100,441	655,078	48,201	2,582			27,450	162						
Williamsburgh	4,397	24,577		7,630	289,713		22,035				1,565						
York	11,813	35,797	64,755	109,691	690,447		6,088	199		219,771							

TABLE LXI.—Concluded.

COUNTIES.	MANUFACTURES. Establishments. Produced in Families.	Annual Product.	Hands Employed.	Capital.	Wine, Gallons.	Value of Orchard Produce.	Value of Produce of Market Gardens.	Value of Animals Slaughtered.	Beeswax and Honey, Pounds.	Silk Cocoons, Pounds.	Wool, Pounds.	Ginned Cotton, Bales of 400 Pounds.	Tobacco, Pounds.	Rice, Pounds.	Molasses, Gallons.
Abbeville	$71,774	$257,133	403	$298,920				$267,864	36,042		28,615	27,192	4,455	7,180	
Anderson	86,705	280,105	233	134,445	1,000	$66		163,485	20,842	100	22,372	6,670	18,540	956,940	55
Barnwell	14,643	226,250	346	179,990				148,717	280		15,996	10,138		7,440	
Beaufort	10,690	59,080	75	63,880	300		$200	121,317	7,975		24,730	12,672		47,230,082	6,621
Charleston	17,799	2,749,961	1,413	1,487,800		2,185	26,940	78,086	1,634		18,634	7,807		16,906,273	
Chester	22,405	101,360	162	104,370	20	4,751		119,304	6,770		8,705	17,810	12	1,110	
Chesterfield	45,080	88,494	213	65,775		7,847	25	67,910	4,790		8,269	3,194	800	42,748	
Colleton	19,240	17,150	58	35,700		495	135	117,157	5,166		25,789	3,006	100	44,102,990	8,520
Darlington	12,070	71,670	126	76,400			705	125,739			9,748	13,005		96,510	25
Edgefield	94,468	635,096	1,064	724,435			1,115	306,825	52,015		34,735	25,880	1,190	12,304	
Fairfield	16,350	44,200	70	19,400	350	2,196		122,360	735		5,562	18,122		4,316	
Georgetown		68,519	74	43,500		15,029	17,073	21,425			22,171	81		46,765,040	
Greenville	28,625	213,510	290	176,850		220	90	104,677	5,724		15,760	2,452	12,505	15,782	
Horry	24,555	130,129	109	59,200			20	75,545			16,672	15	2,379	484,970	483
Kershaw	7,686	127,825	185	100,200		170	340	44,698	1,120		7,102	9,015		74,675	
Lancaster	19,590	46,100	35	36,400		475		74,092	246		10,536	8,661		27,900	
Laurens	54,670	419,715	250	184,475		563		171,337	15,890		19,609	15,842	1,519	128	
Lexington	17,458	176,343	321	249,663	10			72,379	11,420		9,133	4,608	25	50,829	180
Marion	40,624							148,404			18,401	8,680	817	513,825	20
Marlborough	32,674	68,600	79	56,405				78,810	480		9,439	9,501		20,854	
Newberry	35,343	151,145	116	71,810		100		149,701	4,872		14,411	19,894	200	19,427	
Orangeburgh	27,597	67,180	96	58,450				130,446		3	22,332	10,024		1,299,379	
Pickens	68,599	41,192	59	27,923	2,200	43	43	123,070	17,769		19,427	1,357	29,967	28,044	
Richland	4,442	349,964	324	157,920		750	600	82,082	1,636		6,868	11,365		87,970	
Spartanburgh	39,078	173,820	333	265,350				153,706	6,944		22,348	6,671	1,526	3,601	
Sumter	24,248	227,394	180	64,650		210		176,807			6,799	18,799		833,651	
Union	41,897	194,793	227	286,518				135,432	15,023		22,497	14,156			
Williamsburgh	12,825							82,818	46	20	3,928	4,298	100	69	
York	18,290	81,905	186	1,016,606				100,944	19,761		20,545	9,986	150	354,543	

SOLDIERS IN THE REVOLUTIONARY WAR.

The number of men which the several States furnished in the Revolutionary war is shown in the following table, compiled from the Report of the Secretary of War to the House of Representatives, May 10, 1790. The "conjectural militia" served for short periods, — from two months to eight. In Virginia and South Carolina, the aggregate of such militia is increased considerably by the addition of militia raised temporarily to defend the State legislatures while in session.

TABLE LXII.

Statement of the Number of Men furnished by the several States in the Revolutionary War.

FREE STATES.	Number of Continental Troops.	Number of Militia.	Total Continental Troops and Militia.	Conjectural Estimate of Militia.
New Hampshire	12,496	2,093	14,589	3,700
Massachusetts	67,937	15,155	83,092	9,500
Rhode Island	5,908	4,284	10,192	1,500
Connecticut	32,039	7,792	39,831	3,000
New York	17,781	3,312	21,093	8,750
Pennsylvania	25,608	7,357	32,965	2,000
New Jersey	10,727	6,055	16,782	2,500
Total	172,496	46,048	218,544	30,950

TABLE LXII.—*Concluded.*

SLAVE STATES.	Number of Continental Troops.	Number of Militia.	Total Continental Troops and Militia.	Conjectural Estimate of Militia.
Delaware	2,387	376	2,763	1,000
Maryland................	13,912	5,464	19,376	4,000
Virginia.................	26,672	4,163	30,835	21,880
North Carolina...........	7,263	2,716	9,979	12,000
South Carolina...........	5,508	....	5,508	28,000
Georgia	2,679	....	2,679	9,930
Total	58,421	12,719	71,140	76,810

TABLE LXIII.

Number of Pensioners returned by the Census of 1840.

FREE STATES.		SLAVE STATES.	
Maine....................	1,409	Delaware.................	4
New Hampshire	1,408	Maryland.................	95
Massachusetts	2,462	Virginia.................	993
Vermont	1,320	North Carolina............	609
Rhode Island	601	South Carolina............	318
Connecticut	1,666	Georgia	325
New York	4,089	Alabama	192
New Jersey	1,627	Mississippi................	63
Pennsylvania	1,251	Louisiana	12
Ohio.....................	875	Tennessee	895
Indiana	380	Kentucky.................	886
Illinois	195	Missouri	122
Michigan.................	90	Arkansas	24
Wisconsin	9	Florida....................	16
Iowa.....................	2	....	
Total 17,384		Total 4,554	

ACTION AND CONDITION OF SOUTH CAROLINA IN THE
REVOLUTION.

Our first extract in regard to the course of South Carolina
is from a carefully prepared article by Charles C. Hazewell,
Esq., published in the *Boston Daily Chronicle*, August 12,
1856:

The first *Southern* authority that we shall quote, is that of
an actor in the business spoken of — William Moultrie. There
is no purer name connected with the history of our Revolution
than that of Moultrie. He commanded the American forces
that successfully defended the fort on Sullivan's Island, June
28th, 1776, against a strong British squadron — perhaps, all
things considered, the most gallant action of the war, and the
last that was fought, so far as we know, while our country was
still in a formal condition of colonial dependence. The fort
was subsequently named after him. He served with brilliancy
and usefulness subsequently to the date mentioned, and rose to
the rank of major-general in the national service. He was
elevated to the place of Governor of South Carolina, in days
when men thought worthy of that post would sooner have died
than have approved of an attempt to commit murder. In 1802,
Governor Moultrie published, in two volumes, *Memoirs of the
American Revolution, so far as it related to the States of North
and South Carolina, and Georgia*, etc. This is an interesting
work, boldly written and faithfully compiled, and bearing on
every page evidences of the author's ability, integrity, and en-
lightened patriotism. He was, in short, worthy to stand side
by side with Marion, Sumpter, Laurens, and the rest of those
Carolina soldiers who served their country so well, and whose
eminent worth has ever been admitted by all Northern men.
When the British Gen. Prevost (Moultrie calls him *Provost*)
appeared before Charleston, May 11th, 1779, Gen. Moultrie

(130)

was appointed to command the troops in that town, by Governor Rutledge and the council, who were then and there present. He represents the governor to have been much frightened, overrating the enemy's force, and underrating that of the Americans. Governor Rutledge, says Gen. Moultrie, "represented to me the horrors of a storm; he told me that the State's engineer (Col. Senf) had represented to him the lines to be in a very weak state: after some conversation, he proposed to me the sending out a flag, to know what terms we could obtain; I told him, I thought we could stand against the enemy; that I did not think they could force the lines; and that I did not choose to send a flag in my name, but if he chose it, and would call the council together, I would send any message: they requested me to send the following, which was delivered by Mr. Kinloch:

"General Moultrie perceiving from the motions of your army, that your intention is to besiege the town, would be glad to know on what terms you would be disposed to grant a capitulation, should he be inclined to capitulate." (Moultrie's Memoirs, vol. I., p. 427.)

To this message, Gen. Prevost made a reply, full of those promises which the British commanders were so ready to give, and equally ready to break after their enemies had been deluded into placing faith in them. This letter was given to the governor, who called a meeting of the council, at which Moultrie, Pulaski, and Laurens were present. The question of giving up the town was argued, the military men all advising the civilians not to think of surrendering, and showing that the enemy could be beaten off; but Gov. Rutledge would have it that the American force was much exaggerated, and was ready to believe in any statement that exaggerated the British strength. Finally, Gen. Moultrie was authorized to send an answer to Gen. Prevost, refusing to surrender on the latter's terms, but offering, if he would appoint an officer to confer on terms, to send one to meet him, at such time and place as Gen. Prevost might fix on.   Gen. Moultrie says:

"When the question was carried *for giving up the town upon a neutrality,* I will not say who was for the question but this I well remember, that Mr. John Edwards, one of the privy council, a worthy citizen, and a very respectable merchant of Charleston, was so affected as to weep, and said, ' What, are we to give up the town at last? '

" The governor and council adjourned to Colonel Beekman's tent on the lines, at the gate.   I sent for Colonel John Laurens from his house, to request the favor he would carry a message from the governor and council to General Prevost; but when he knew the purpose, he begged to be excused from carrying such a message that it was much against his inclination ; that he would do anything to serve his country; but he could not think of carrying such a message as that!   I then sent for Colonel M'Intosh, and requested he would go with Colonel Roger Smith, who was called on by the governor, with the message; they both begged I would excuse them; hoped, and requested I would get some other person.   I, however, pressed them into a compliance; which message was as follows:

" ' *I propose a neutrality during the war between* Great Britain and America, *and the question,* WHETHER THE STATE SHALL BELONG TO GREAT BRITAIN, OR REMAIN ONE OF THE UNITED STATES ? *be determined by the treaty of peace between those two powers.'* "   (Memoirs, Vol. I., pp. 432–33.

John Marshall, so long Chief Justice of the United States Supreme Court, a Virginian by birth, and a man of the highest reputation, has given a brief account of what happened at Charleston after Prevost's arrival before it.   "The town was summoned to surrender," he says, "and the day was spent in sending and receiving flags. *The neutrality of South Carolina, during the war, leaving the question whether that State should finally belong to Great Britain or the United States* to be settled in the treaty of peace, was proposed by the garrison and rejected by Prevost.".   (Marshall's Life of Washington, vol. I. pp. 298–9, Phil. ed., 1832.)

Among the historians of the American Revolution is Dr. Ramsay, of South Carolina, whose history was published in

1789. In his account of what happened at Charleston, after Gen Prevost's arrival before that place, occurs the following passage : " Commissioners from the garrison were instructed to *propose a neutrality during the war between Great Britain and America*, and that the question whether the State shall belong to Great Britain, or remain one of the United States, be decided by the treaty of peace between these powers." The British commanders refused this advantageous offer, alleging that they had not come in a legislative capacity, and insisted that, as the inhabitants and others were in arms, they should surrender prisoners of war. (Ramsay, p. 425.)

The last authority we shall quote is Professor Bowen.* After mentioning the proposal made to the British commander, he comments on it as follows :

" This proposal did not come merely from the commander of a military garrison, in which case, of course, it would have been only nugatory ; the governor of the State, clothed with discretionary powers, was in the place, and probably most of his council along with him. Whether such a proposition would have been justifiable under any circumstances is a question that needs not be discussed ; at any rate, it would not have evinced much honorable or patriotic feeling. But to make such an offer in the present case was conduct little short of treason. Till within a fortnight, not an enemy's foot had pressed their ground ; and even now, the British held no strong position, had captured none of their forts, and occupied only the little space actually covered by the army in front of the town. The garrison equalled this army in strength, and might safely bid it defiance. No succors were at hand for the British, while the certain arrival of Lincoln within a week would place them between two fires, and make their position eminently hazardous. Yet, with these prospects before them, the authorities of the place made a proposition, which was equivalent *to an offer from the State to return to its allegiance to the British crown*. The transaction deserves particular notice here, because the surrender of Charleston, in the following year, a surrender brought about by the prevalence of the same unpatriotic feelings, was made the ground of some very unjust reflections on the conduct of Lincoln, their military commander." (Life of Benjamin Lincoln, in Spark's American Biography, Sec. Ser., vol. XIII., pp. 285–6 "

* Of Harvard University.

This was the action of South Carolina in 1779. In the early part of the next year, a British force under Sir Henry Clinton appeared before Charleston, and on the first day of April broke ground within half a mile of the American works. Clinton was aided by a naval force under Vice Admiral Arbuthnot. The American forces in Charleston were some 2,000 regulars, and twice as many militia and armed citizens, under the command of Gen. Lincoln.

On the 10th of April, 1780, the British commanders sent to Gen. Lincoln a summons to surrender the city of Charleston, to which Lincoln promptly returned the following answer (which, with the other papers in this chapter relating to the doings of the year 1780, we take from " Almon's Remembrancer," a work of 17 vols., published in London during the Revolutionary war. The work is extremely rare, and the copy which we use is that belonging to Harvard University) :

" *To Gen. Sir* HENRY CLINTON, *and Vice Admiral* ARBUTHNOT, *etc. :*

" GENTLEMEN, — I have received your summons of this date. Sixty days have passed since it was known that your intentions against this town were hostile, in which, time has been afforded to abandon it; but duty and inclination point to the propriety of supporting it to the last extremity.

" I have the honour to be, etc.,
                    (Signed,)   " B. LINCOLN,
                              " *Commander in the South Department.*
" CHARLES-TOWN, April 10, 1780."

On the 8th of May, a second summons was sent by Gen. Clinton, to which the following answer was returned:

" *To his Excellency, Sir* HENRY CLINTON :

" SIR, — The same motives of humanity which inclined you to propose articles of capitulation to this garrison, induced me to offer those I had the honour of sending you on the 8th instant. [In answer to Clinton's summons of the 8th, Lincoln had proposed terms of capitulation, which had been rejected by the British commander. Reference is here made by Gen. Lincoln to the rejected terms.] They then appeared to me such as I might proffer, and you receive, with honor to both parties. Your exceptions to them, as they *principally concerned the militia and citizens*, I then conceived were such as could not be concurred with; BUT A RECENT APPLICATION FROM THOSE PEOPLE, *wherein they express a willingness to comply with them*, and a wish on my part to lessen, as much as may be, the distresses of war to individuals, lead me now to offer you my acceptance of them.

"I have the honour to be, etc., .

(Signed,) "B. LINCOLN.

"CHARLES-TOWN, May 11, 1780."

[The terms were, the Continental troops to be held as prisoners of war, the militia and citizens prisoners on parole, the town and fortifications to be surrendered without change, etc.]

To show the feelings of the people of South Carolina after the surrender of Charleston, we give the following extract of a letter from Sir Henry Clinton to Lord George Germaine, one of his majesty's principal secretaries of state, dated "Head-Quarters, Charlestown, South Carolina, June 4, 1730:"

"With the greatest pleasure I further report to your Lordship, that the inhabitants from every quarter repair to the detachments of the army, and to this garrison, to declare their allegiance to the King, and to offer their services in arms in support of his government. In many instances they have brought prisoners, their former oppressors, or leaders; and I may venture to assert, that there are few men in South Carolina who are not either our prisoners, or in arms with us." — *Almon's Rem., vol.* x., *p.* 76.

The following petition is to the same effect. It is found in the work before quoted, vol. x., pp. 83, 186:

"*To their Excellencies, Sir* HENRY CLINTON, *Knight of the Bath, General of his Majesty's forces, and* MARIOT ARBUTHNOT, *Esq., Vice Admiral of the Blue, his Majesty's Commissioners to restore peace and good government in the several colonies in rebellion in North America:*

"THE HUMBLE ADDRESS OF DIVERS INHABITANTS OF CHARLES-TOWN:

"The inhabitants of Charles-Town, by the articles of capitulation are declared prisoners on parole; but we the underwritten, having every inducement to return to our allegiance, and ardently hoping speedily to be re-admitted to the character and condition of British subjects, take this opportunity of tendering to your Excellencies our warmest congratulations on *the restoration of this capital and Province to their political connection with the Crown and Government of Great Britain;* an event which will add lustre to your Excellencies' characters, and, we trust, entitle you to the most distinguishing mark of the Royal favour. Although the right of taxing America, in Parliament, excited considerable ferments in the minds of the people of this Province, yet it may, with a religious adherance to truth, be affirmed, that they did not entertain the most distant thought of dissolving the union which so happily subsisted between them and their parent country; and when, in the progress of that fatal controversy, the *doctrine of* INDEPENDENCY, *which originated in the more* NORTHERN COLONIES, made its appearance among us, our nature revolted at the idea, and we look back with the most painful regret on those convulsions that gave existence to a power of subverting a Constitution, for which we always had, and ever shall retain, the most profound veneration, and substituting in its stead a *rank democracy,* which, however carefully digested in theory, on being reduced into practice, has exhibited a system of tyrannic domination only to be found among the uncivilized part of mankind, or in the history of the dark and barbarous ages of antiquity.

" We sincerely lament, that *after the repeal of those statutes which gave rise to the troubles in America, the overtures made by his Majesty's Commissioners, from time to time, were not regarded by our late rulers.* To this fatal inattention are to be attributed those calamities which have *involved our country in a state of misery and ruin,* from which, however, we trust, it will soon emerge, by the wisdom and clemency of his Majesty's auspicious Government, and the influence of prudential laws, adapted to the nature of the evils we labour under; and that the people will be restored to those privileges, in the enjoyment whereof their former felicity consisted.

" Animated with these hopes, we entreat your Excellencies' interposition, in assuring his Majesty, that we shall glory in every occasion of manifesting that zeal and affection for his person and government, with which gratitude can inspire a free and joyful people.

" CHARLES-TOWN, June 5, 1780.

(Signed,)

John Wragg,	James Cook,	Gideon Dupont, jr.,
William Glinn,	Chr. Fitz-Simmons,	Jer. Savage,
John Stopton,	John Davis,	Andrew Reid,
John Rose,	Benj. Baker, sen.,	Zeph. Kingsby,
Wm. Greenwood,	John Fisher,	Alex. Oliphant,
Jacob Vulk,	Charles Atkins,	Paul Hamilton,

Robert Wilson,
Leonard Askew,
And. McKensie,
Rob. Lithgow,
Wm. Wayne,
Ja. G. Williams,
James Ross,
John Moncrief,
John Wells, jun.,
Allard Bellin,
John Wogner,
John Ward Taylor,
Jock Holmes,
James Megown,
Wm. Davie,
James Duming,
John Sprisd,
Wm. Nervcob,
John Daniel,
John Collum,
John Smith,
Lewis Dutarque,
James McKlown,
Wm. Burt,
John Watson,
Anthony Montell,
James Lynch,
George Grant,
Abraham Pearce,
John Miot,
Fred. Augustine,
John Webb,
Robert Williams,
Alex. Macbeth,
John Robertson,
John Liber,
Hugh Rose,
Patrick Bower,
Thomas Tod,
Brian Foskie,
Thomas Eustace,
Emanuel Marshall,

And. Mitchell,
Farq. McCollum,
George Adamson,
· William Valentine,
Christo. Williman,
D. Pendergrass,
Daniel Bell,
Edw. Cure,
Thomas Timms,
Thomas Buckle, sen.,
Hopkins Price,
George Denholm,
Roger Brown,
James Strictland,
Wm. McKimmy,
Michael Hubert,
David Bruce,
John Gray,
Tho. Dawson,
Tho. Winstanly,
Cha. Ramadge,
Wm. Bower,
Alex. Walker,
John Lyon,
Robert Philip,
Robert Johnson,
David Taylor,
John Latuff,
John Gillsnoez,
John Barson,
Ja. Donavan, jun.,
Nicholas Boden,
Ja. McKensie,
Henry Walsh,
Isaac Clarke,
John Durst,
William Cameron,
John Russell,
John Bell,
John Hayes,
James McKie,
James Gillandeau,

Ch. Bouchomeau,
John Bury,
Daniel Boyne,
Peter Lambert,
Hen. Bookless,
Wm. Edwards,
Tho. Buckle, jun.,
Henry Ephram,
John Hartly,
James Carmichael,
Samuel Adams,
Chr. Shutts,
Alex. Smith,
John McCall,
John Abercrombie,
Joseph Jones,
Henry Branton,
John Callagan,
John Ralph,
Samuel Bower,
George Young,
Jos. Milligan,
Anthony Geaubeau,
William Smith,
Jas. Robertson,
Michael Quin,
John Gornley,
Walter Rosewell,
Richard Dennis,
John W. Gibbs,
Benj. Sinker,
John Bartels,
Wm. Miller,
John Burges,
Thomas Hutchinson,
Thomas Else,
Alex. Harvey,
John Pafford,
Tho. Phepoe,
Samuel Knight,
Archibald Carson,
Tho. Elliott,

Thomas Clary,
Tho. Hooper,
Ch. Sutter,
Robert Lindsey,
Tho. Richardson,
James Rach,
Peter Dumont,
Tho. Saunders,
Ed. Legge,
Henry Hardroff,
Aaron Locoock,
Arch. Brown,
Wm. Russell,
Thomas Coram,
James Hartley,
Andrew Thompson,
William Layton,
Nich. Smith,
Andrew Stewart,
John Hartley,
Tho. Stewart,

Hugh Truir,
Lewis Coffere,
Hugh Kirkham,
Wm. Farrow,
Wm. Arisam,
Tho. Deighton,
Robert Paterson,
John Parkinson,
John Love,
Alex. Ingles,
William Mills,
James Duncan,
Ja. Blackburn,
John Johnston,
Samuel Perry,
Geo. R. Williams,
Matthias Hunkin,
Edm. Petrie,
Wm. Nisbett,
Geo. Cook,
Peter Procue,

Gilbert Chaliner,
Arch. Downs,
Alex. Johnstone,
James Fagan,
Ja. Bryant,
James Courtonque,
Joseph Wyatt,
John Cuple,
James McLinachus,
Wm. Jennings,
Patrick McKam,
Robt. Beard,
Stephen Townshend,
Ja. Snead,
Ch. Burnham,
Rob. McIntosh,
Charles H. Simonds,
G. Thompson,
Isaac Lessence,
Isaac Manych."

The following is a part of Benedict Arnold's Address to the inhabitants of America, justifying *his* treason. The Address appeared in the *New-York Gazette* of Nov. 11, 1780. We copy from "Almon's Remembrancer," vol. x. p. 344. The reader will note the similarity of language and reasoning to that used by the "210* principal inhabitants" of the capital of South Carolina :

"*To the Inhabitants of America :*

"I should forfeit, even in my own opinion, the place I have so long held in yours, if I could be indifferent to your approbation, and silent on the motives which have induced me to join the King's arms. A very few words, however, shall suffice on a subject so personal ; for, to the thousands *who suffer under the tyranny of the usurpers in the revolted* PROVINCES, as well as to the great multitude who have long wished for its subversion, this instance of my conduct can want no vindication, and as *to the class of men who are criminally protracting the war from sinister views, at the expense of the public interest,* I prefer their enmity to their applause. * * *

"When I quitted domestic happiness for the perils of the field, I con-

* In the list which we copy, 206.

ceived the rights of my country in danger, and that duty and honor called me to her defence. A redress of grievances was my only object and aim; however, *I acquiesced in a step which I thought precipitate, the Declaration of Independence; to justify this measure, many plausible reasons were urged, which could no longer exist, when Great Britain, with the open arms of a parent, offered to embrace us as children, and grant the wished-for redress.*

* * * * "With respect to that herd of censurers, whose enmity to me originates in their hatred to the principles by which I am now led to devote my life to the re-union of the British Empire, as the best and only means to dry up *the streams of misery that have deluged this country,* they may be assured, that, conscious of the rectitude of my intention, I shall treat their malice and calumnies with contempt and neglect.

"B. ARNOLD.

"NEW YORK, October 7, 1780."

On the same 5th day of June, 1780, when the principal inhabitants of South Carolina were petitioning to be " re-admitted to the character and condition of British subjects," and offering their " congratulations on the restoration of their capital and *province* to their political connection with the crown and government of Great Britain,"-the following is the brief record of Massachusetts (" Almon's Remembrancer," vol. x. p. 193) :

"BOSTON, June 5.

" Wednesday being the anniversary for the election of Counsellors, the General Assembly met at the State-House, and, *after the oath of allegiance to the* STATE *was administered to the gentlemen returned from the several towns, to serve as members of the Hon. House of Representatives,* they unanimously made choice of Hon. JOHN HANCOCK, Esq., for Speaker, and Samuel Freeman, Esq., for their Clerk. The two Houses, escorted by the Independent Company of this town, then proceeded to the old Brick Meeting-House, where an excellent sermon was preached by the Rev. Mr. Howard, from Exodus xviii. 21."

Of this House of Representatives, it may be further said, that it numbered one hundred and seventy-six members; a number not quite so large as the two hundred and ten South Carolinians. In this list of Representatives, appear the names of *Hancock, Austin, Lowell, Phillips, Parker, Sedgwick, Prescott, Pickering,* etc.

CHAPTER XIII.

THE LAWS OF KANSAS.

THAT our readers may understand exactly what the laws are which the free State men in Kansas are now threatened with death for disobeying, we present such portions of the statute book of that Territory as relate especially to the institution of slavery. The public must judge whether or not the laws deserve the epithets, "outrageous," "unconstitutional," "disgraceful," lately bestowed on them by Mr. Cass, Mr. Geyer, and Mr. Weller. The title of the volume from which we quote, is: "The Statutes of the Territory of Kansas, passed at the first Session of the Legislative Assembly, one thousand eight hundred and fifty-five. To which are affixed, the Declaration of Independence, and the Constitution of the United States, and the Act of Congress organizing said Territory, and other Acts of Congress having immediate relation thereto. Printed in pursuance of the statute in such cases made and provided. Shawnee M. L. School: John T. Brady, Public Printer. 1855."* Pp. 1058.

ELECTIONS. — (Chapter 66, section 11, page 332.)

Every free white male citizen of the United States, and every free male Indian, who is made a citizen, by treaty or oth-

---

* This volume is extremely rare. There is thought to be but one copy in New England — the one we have used — which belongs to Dr. T. H. Webb, of the Emigrant Aid Company. At the treaty, recently made by Gov. Shannon with the free State men at Lawrence, it was one of the stipulations that two copies of this work should be furnished the people of Lawrence. We have not learned whether the governor keeps his promises as well as usual.

erwise, and over the age of twenty-one years, who shall be an inhabitant of this Territory, and of the county or district in which he offers to vote, and shall have paid a Territorial tax, shall be a qualified elector for all elective officers; and all Indians who are inhabitants of this Territory, and who may have adopted the customs of the white man, and who are liable to pay taxes, shall be deemed citizens ; *Provided,* that no soldier, seaman, or marine, in the regular army or navy of the United States, shall be entitled to vote by being on service therein; *And provided further,* that no person who shall have been convicted of any violation of any of the provisions of an act of Congress, entitled, " An act respecting fugitives from justice, and persons escaping from the service of their masters," approved February 12th, 1793 ; or of an act to amend and supplementary to said act, approved 18th September, 1850; whether such conviction were by criminal proceeding, or by civil action for the recovery of any penalty prescribed by either of said acts, in any court of the United States, or any State or Territory, of any offence deemed infamous, shall be entitled to vote at any election, or to hold any office in this Territory ; *And provided further,* that if any person offering to vote shall be challenged and required to take an oath or affirmation, to be administered by one of the judges of the election, that he will sustain the provisions of the above recited acts of Congress, and of the act entitled, " An act to organize the Territories of Nebraska and Kansas," approved May 30, 1854, and shall refuse to take such oath or affirmation, the vote of such person shall be rejected.

Sec. 12. Every person possessing the qualification of a voter, as herein above prescribed, and who shall have resided in this Territory thirty days prior to the election at which he may offer himself as a candidate, shall be eligible as a delegate to the house of representatives of the United States, to either branch of the legislative assembly, and to all other offices in this territory, not otherwise especially provided for ; *Provided*

13

however, that each member of the legislative assembly, and every officer elected or appointed to office under the laws of this territory, shall, in addition to the oath or affirmation specially provided to be taken by such officer, take an oath or affirmation to support the constitution of the United States, the provisions of an act, entitled, " An act respecting fugitives from justice and persons escaping from the service of their masters," approved February 12, 1793; and of an act to amend and supplementary to said last mentioned act, approved September 18th, 1850; and of an act, entitled, " An act to organize the Territories of Nebraska and Kansas," approved May 30, 1854.

Officers. —(Chapter 117, section 1, page 516.)

All officers elected or appointed under any existing or subsequently enacted laws of this Territory, shall take and subscribe the following oath of office : " I ———— do solemnly swear, upon the holy Evangelists of Almighty God, that I will *support* the Constitution of the United States, and that I will *support and sustain* the provisions of an act, entitled, ' An act to organize the Territories of Nebraska and Kansas,' and the provisions of the law of the United States, commonly known as the ' *Fugitive Slave Law,*' and faithfully and impartially, and to the best of my ability, demean myself in the discharge of my duties in the office of ————; so help me God."

Jurors. — (Chapter 92, section 13, page 444.)

No person who is conscientiously opposed to the holding of slaves, or who does not admit the right to hold slaves in this Territory, shall be a juror in any cause in which the right to hold any person in slavery is involved, nor in any cause in which any injury done to or committed by any slave is in issue, nor in any criminal proceeding for the violation of any law enacted for the protection of slave property and for the punishment of crimes committed against the right to such property.

ATTORNEYS AT LAW. — (Chapter 11, section 3, page 132.)

Every person obtaining a license (to practice law) shall take an oath, or affirmation, to support the Constitution of the United States, and to support and sustain the provisions of an act, entitled, "An act to organize the Territories of Nebraska and Kansas," and the provisions of an act, commonly known as the "Fugitive Slave Law," and faithfully to demean himself in his practice, to the best of his knowledge and ability. A certificate of such oath shall be endorsed on the license.

SLAVES. — (Chapter 151 ; page 715.)

An Act to punish offences against slave property.

SECTION 1. Be it enacted, by the Governor and Legislative Assembly of the Territory of Kansas, That every person, bond or free, who shall be convicted of actually raising a rebellion, or insurrection of slaves, free negroes or mulattoes, in this Territory, shall suffer death.

SEC. 2. Every free person, who shall aid and assist in any rebellion or insurrection of slaves, free negroes, or mulattoes, or shall furnish arms, or do any overt act in furtherance of such rebellion or insurrection, shall suffer death.

SEC. 3. If any free person shall, by speaking, writing, or printing, advise, persuade, or induce any slaves to rebel, conspire against, or murder any citizen of this Territory, or shall bring into, print, write, publish, or circulate, or cause to be brought into, printed, written, published, or circulated, or shall knowingly aid or assist in the bringing into, printing, writing, publishing, or circulating in this Territory, any book, paper, magazine, pamphlet or circular, for the purpose of exciting insurrection on the part of the slaves, free negroes, or mulattoes, against the Territory, or any part of them, such person shall be guilty of felony and suffer death.

SEC. 4. If any person shall entice, decoy, or carry away out of this Territory, any slaves belonging to another, with the intent to deprive the owner thereof of the services of such slaves, or with intent to effect or procure the freedom of such slave, he shall be adjudged guilty of grand larceny, and, on conviction thereof, shall suffer death, or be imprisoned at hard labor for not less than ten years.

SEC. 5. If any person aids or assists in enticing, decoying, or persuading, or carrying away, or sending out of this Territory, any slave belonging to another, with intent to procure or effect the freedom of such slave, or with intent to deprive the owner thereof of the services of such slave, he shall be adjudged guilty of grand larceny, and, on conviction thereof, shall suffer death, or be imprisoned at hard labor for not less than ten years.

SEC. 6. If any person shall entice, decoy, or carry away out of any State or other Territory of the United States, any slave belonging to another, with intent to procure or effect the freedom of such slave, or to deprive the owner thereof of the services of such slave, and shall bring such slave into this Territory, he shall be adjudged guilty of grand larceny, in the same manner as if such slave had been enticed, decoyed, or carried away out of the Territory, and in such case the larceny may be charged to have been committed in any county of this Territory, into or through which such slave shall have been brought by such person, and, on conviction thereof, the person offending shall suffer death, or be imprisoned at hard labor for not less than ten years.

SEC. 7. If any person shall entice, persuade, or induce any slave to escape from the service of his master or owner in this Territory, or shall aid or assist any slave escaping from the service of his master or owner, or shall assist, harbor, or conceal any slave who may have escaped from the service of his master or owner, he shall be deemed guilty of felony, and punished by imprisonment at hard labor for not less than five years.

SEC. 8. If any person in this Territory shall aid or assist, harbor, or conceal any slave who has escaped from the service of his master or owner in another State or Territory, such person shall be punished in like manner as if such slave had escaped from the service of his master or owner in this Territory.

SEC. 9. If any person shall resist any officer while attempting to arrest any slave that may have escaped from the service of his master or owner, or shall rescue such slaves when in custody of any officer or other person, or shall entice, persuade, aid, or assist such slave to escape from the custody of any officer, or other person who may have such slave in custody, whether such slave has escaped from the service of his master or owner in this Territory or in any other State or Territory, the person so offending shall be guilty of felony, and punished by imprisonment at hard labor for a term not less than two years.

. SEC. 10. If any Marshal, Sheriff, or Constable, or the Deputy of any such officer, shall, when required by any person, refuse to aid or assist in the arrest and capture of any slave that may have escaped from the service of his master or owner, whether such slave shall have escaped from his master or owner in this Territory or any other State or Territory, such officer shall be fined in a sum of not less than one hundred nor more than five hundred dollars.

SEC. 11. If any person print, write, introduce into, publish, or circulate, or cause to be brought into, printed, written, published, or circulated, or shall knowingly aid or assist in bringing into, printing, publishing, or circulating within this Territory, any book, paper, pamphlet, magazine, handbill, or circular, containing any statements, arguments, opinions, sentiment, doctrine, advice, or inuendo, calculated to produce a disorderly, dangerous or rebellious disaffection among the slaves in this Territory, or to induce such slaves to escape from the service of their masters, or resist their authority, he shall be guilty of felony, and be punished by imprisonment at hard labor for a term not less than five years.

13*

SEC. 12. If any free person, by speaking or writing, assert or maintain that persons have not the right to hold slaves in this Territory, or shall introduce into this Territory, print, publish, write, circulate, or cause to be written, printed, published, or circulated in this Territory, any book, paper, magazine, pamphlet, or circular containing any denial of the right of such persons to hold slaves in this Territory, such person shall be deemed guilty of felony, and punished by imprisonment at hard labor for a term not less than two years.

SEC. 13. No person who is conscientiously opposed to holding slaves, or who does not admit the right to hold slaves in this Territory, shall sit as a juror on the trial of any prosecution for the violation of any of the sections of this act.

This act to take effect and be in force from and after the 15th day of September, A. D. 1855.

Chapter 152, page 718.

An Act giving meaning to the word "State."

SEC. 1. Wherever the word "State" occurs in any act of the present Legislative Assembly, or any law of the Territory, in such construction as to indicate the locality of the operation of such act or laws, the same shall in every instance be taken and understood to mean "Territory," and shall apply to the Territory of Kansas.

APPENDIX.

[We give in this Appendix the original Tables of the Census Compendium, with some other Tables referred to in the text.]

(152)

TABLE I.

Aggregate Population and Density of the States and Territories.

STATES.	POPULATION.							DENSITY.	
	1790.	1800.	1810.	1820.	1830.	1840.	1850.	1840.	1850.
Alabama				c 127,901	300,527	590,756	771,623	11.65	15.21
Arkansas				14,273	30,388	97,574	209,897	1.87	4.02
California							92,597		.59
Columbia, District of		14,093	24,023	33,089	39,834	43,712	51,687	437.12	861.45
Connecticut	238,141	251,002	262,042	275,202	297,675	309,978	370,792	66.32	79.33
Delaware	59,096	64,273	72,674	72,749	76,748	78,085	91,532	36.83	43.13
Florida					34,730	54,477	87,445	0.92	1.43
Georgia	82,548	162,101	252,433	340,987	516,823	691,392	906,185	11.93	15.62
Illinois			12,282	55,211	157,445	476,183	851,470	8.59	15.37
Indiana		4,875	24,520	147,178	343,031	685,866	988,416	20.28	29.24
Iowa						43,112	192,214	0.85	3.73
Kentucky	73,077	220,955	406,511	564,317	687,917	779,828	982,405	20.70	26.07
Louisiana			76,556	153,407	215,739	352,411	517,762	8.54	12.55
Maine	96,540	151,719	228,705	298,335	399,455	501,793	583,169	15.80	18.36
Maryland	319,728	341,548	380,546	407,350	447,040	470,019	583,034	42.25	52.41
Massachusetts	378,717	423,245	472,040	523,287	610,408	737,699	994,514	94.58	127.50
Michigan			4,762	8,896	31,639	212,267	397,654	3.77	7.07
Mississippi		8,850	40,352	75,448	136,621	375,651	606,326	7.97	12.86
Missouri			20,845	66,586	140,455	383,702	682,044	5.69	10.12
New Hampshire	141,899	183,762	214,360	244,161	269,328	284,574	317,976	30.67	34.26
New Jersey	184,139	211,949	245,555	277,575	320,823	373,306	489,555	44.87	58.84
New York	340,120	586,756	959,049	1,372,812	1,918,608	2,428,921	3,097,394	51.68	65.90
North Carolina	393,751	478,103	555,500	638,829	737,987	753,419	869,039	14.86	17.14
Ohio		45,365	230,760	581,494	937,903	1,519,467	1,980,329	38.02	49.55
Pennsylvania	434,373	602,361	810,091	1,049,458	1,348,233	1,724,033	2,311,786	37.48	50.26
Rhode Island	69,110	69,122	77,031	83,059	97,199	108,830	147,545	83.33	112.97
South Carolina	249,073	345,591	415,115	502,741	581,185	594,398	668,507	20.23	22.75

TABLE I — Continued.

Aggregate Population and Density of the States and Territories.

STATES.	POPULATION.							DENSITY.	
	1790.	1800.	1810.	1820.	1830.	1840.	1850.	1840.	1850.
Tennessee	35,791	105,602	261,727	422,813	681,904	829,210	1,002,717	18.18	21.99
Texas							212,592	......	0.89
Vermont	85,416	154,465	217,713	235,764	280,652	291,948	314,120	28.59	30.76
Virginia	748,308	880,200	974,622	1,065,379	1,211,405	1,239,797	1,421,661	20.21	23.17
Wisconsin						30,945	305,391	0.57	5.66
TERRITORIES.									
Minnesota							6,077	......	0.04
New Mexico							61,547	......	0.30
Oregon							13,294	......	0.07
Utah							11,380	......	0.04
		5,305,987 *a* Less 12		9,688,191 *a* Less 60	*b* 5,318	*b* 6,100			
Total	3,929,827	5,305,925	7,239,814	9,688,131	12,866,020	17,069,453	23,191,876	9.55	7.90

a Deducted to make the totals published incorrectly in those years. *b* Persons on board vessels of war in the United States naval service. *c* A later statement from the State Department, for the same year, gave Alabama a total of 144,317.

AGGREGATE NUMBER OF THE WHITE POPULATION OF THE UNITED STATES.—The number of white persons in the United States, on the 1st of June, 1850, was ascertained to be 19,553,068, of whom 17,312,533 were native and 2,240,535 foreign born. By reference to the following table, the aggregate number, at every census, in the States and Territories, will be seen:

TABLE II.

White Population of the United States.

STATES.	1790.	1800.	1810.	1820.	1830.	1840.	1850.
Alabama				85,451	190,406	335,185	426,514
Arkansas				12,579	25,671	77,174	162,189
California							91,635
Columbia, Dist.		10,066	16,079	22,614	27,563	30,657	37,941
Connecticut	232,581	244,721	255,279	267,161	289,603	301,856	363,099
Delaware	46,310	49,852	55,361	55,282	57,601	58,561	71,169
Florida					18,385	27,943	47,203
Georgia	52,886	101,678	145,414	189,566	296,806	407,695	521,572
Illinois			11,501	53,788	155,061	472,254	846,034
Indiana		4,577	23,890	145,758	339,399	678,698	977,154
Iowa						42,924	191,881
Kentucky	61,133	179,871	324,237	434,644	517,787	590,253	761,413
Louisiana			34,311	73,383	89,441	158,457	255,491
Maine	96,002	150,901	227,736	297,340	398,263	500,438	581,813
Maryland	208,649	216,326	235,117	260,223	291,108	318,204	417,943
Massachusetts	373,254	416,793	465,303	516,419	603,359	729,030	985,450
Michigan			4,618	8,591	31,346	211,560	395,071
Mississippi		5,179	23,024	42,176	70,443	179,074	295,718
Missouri			17,227	55,988	114,795	323,888	592,004
New Hampshire	141,111	182,898	213,390	243,236	268,721	284,036	317,456
New Jersey	169,954	195,125	226,861	257,409	300,266	351,588	465,509
New York	314,142	556,039	918,699	1,332,744	1,873,663	2,378,890	3,048,325
North Carolina	288,204	337,764	376,410	419,200	472,843	484,870	553,028
Ohio			228,861	576,572	928,329	1,502,122	1,955,050
Pennsylvania	424,099	586,094	786,804	1,017,094	1,309,900	1,676,115	2,258,160
Rhode Island	64,689	65,437	73,314	79,413	93,621	105,587	143,875
South Carolina	140,178	196,255	214,196	237,440	257,863	259,084	274,563
Tennessee	32,013	91,709	215,875	339,927	535,746	640,627	756,836
Texas							154,034
Vermont	85,144	153,908	216,963	234,846	279,771	291,218	313,402
Virginia	442,115	514,280	551,534	603,087	694,300	740,858	894,800
Wisconsin						30,749	304,756
TERRITORIES.							
Minnesota							6,038
New Mexico							61,525
Oregon							13,087
Utah							11,330
					† 5,318	† 6,100	
		4,304,501 *less 12		7,861,931 *add 6			
Total	3,172,464	4,304,489	5,862,004	7,861,987	10,537,378	14,195,695	19,553,068

* Added or deducted to make the aggregates, published incorrectly in those years.
† Persons on board vessels of war in the United States naval service.

TABLE III.

Free Colored Population of the United States.

STATES.	1790.	1800.	1810.	1820.	1830.	1840.	1850.
Alabama	....	....	....	571	1,572	2,039	2,265
Arkansas........	....	....	....	59	141	• 465	608
California........	....	....	....	....	....	....	962
Columbia, Dist. of	....	783	2,549	4,048	6,152	8,361	10,059
Connecticut......	2,801	5,330	6,453	7,844	8,047	8,105	7,693
Delaware	3,899	8,268	13,136	12,958	15,855	16,919	18,073
Florida	....	....	....	....	844	817	932
Georgia..........	398	1,019	1,801	1,763	2,486	2,753	2,931
Illinois	....	....	613	457	1,637	3,598	5,436
Indiana..........	....	163	393	1,230	3,629	7,165	11,262
Iowa	....	....	....	....	....	172	333
Kentucky........	114	741	1,713	2,759	4,917	7,317	10,011
Louisiana........	....	....	7,585	10,476	16,710	25,502	17,462
Maine	538	818	969	929	1,190	1,355	1,356
Maryland........	8,043	19,587	33,927	39,730	52,938	62,078	74,723
Massachusetts ...	5,463	6,452	6,737	6,740	7,048	8,669	9,064
Michigan	....	....	120	174	261	707	2,583
Mississippi	....	182	240	458	519	1,366	930
Missouri	....	....	607	347	569	1,574	2,618
New Hampshire ..	630	856	970	786	604	537	520
New Jersey	2,762	4,402	7,843	12,460	18,303	21,044	23,810
New York........	4,654	10,374	25,333	29,279	44,870	50,027	49,069
North Carolina...	4,975	7,043	10,266	14,612	19,543	22,732	27,463
Ohio	....	337	1,899	4,723	9,568	17,342	25,279
Pennsylvania	6,537	14,561	22,492	30,202	37,930	47,854	53,626
Rhode Island.....	3,469	3,304	3,609	3,554	3,561	3,238	3,670
South Carolina...	1,801	3,185	4,554	6,826	7,921	8,276	8,960
Tennessee	361	309	1,317	2,727	4,555	5,524	6,422
Texas	....	....	....	....	....	....	397
Vermont	255	557	750	903	881	730	718
Virginia	12,766	20,124	30,570	36,889	47,348	49,852	54,333
Wisconsin	....	....	....	....	....	185	635
TERRITORIES.			•				
Minnesota	....	....	....	....	....	....	39
New Mexico	....	....	....	....	....	....	22
Oregon	....	....	....	....	....	....	207
Utah	....	....	....	....	....	....	24
				233,504 add 20			
Aggregate	59,466	108,395	186,446	233,524	319,599	386,303	434,495

Aggregate Number. — The number of slaves in the United States in 1850, was 3,204,313. The number in each of the States at this and every previous census will be found in the following table

TABLE IV.

Slave Population of the United States.

STATES.	1790.	1800.	1810.	1820.	1830.	1840.	1850.
Alabama	....	....	....	41,879	117,549	253,532	342,844
Arkansas......	....	....	....	1,617	4,576	19,935	47,100
California......	....	....	....	....	....	....	....
Columbia, Dist.	....	3,244	5,395	6,377	6,119	4,694	3,687
Connecticut ...	2,759	951	310	97	25	17	....
Delaware	8,887	6,153	4,177	4,509	3,292	2,605	2,290
Florida........	....	....	....	....	15,501	25,717	39,310
Georgia	29,264	59,404	105,218	149,654	217,531	280,944	381,682
Illinois........	....	....	168	917	747	331	....
Indiana	....	135	237	190	3	3	....
Iowa..........	....	....	....	....	....	16	....
Kentucky	11,830	40,343	80,561	126,732	165,213	182,258	210,981
Louisiana	....	....	34,660	69,064	109,588	168,452	244,809
Maine.........	....	....	....	....	2	....	....
Maryland......	103,036	105,635	111,502	107,397	102,994	89,737	90,368
Massachusetts .	....	....	....	....	1	....	....
Michigan	....	....	24	....	32	....	....
Mississippi	....	3,489	17,088	32,814	65,659	195,211	309,878
Missouri	....	....	3,011	10,222	25,091	58,240	87,422
New Hampshire	158	8	....	....	3	1	....
New Jersey....	11,423	12,422	10,851	7,557	2,254	674	236
New York	21,324	20,343	15,017	10,088	75	4	....
North Carolina	100,572	133,296	168,824	205,017	245,601	245,817	288,548
Ohio..........	....	....	....	....	6	3	....
Pennsylvania ..	3,737	1,706	795	211	403	64	....
Rhode Island ..	952	381	108	48	17	5	....
South Carolina	107,094	146,151	196,365	258,475	315,401	327,038	384,984
Tennessee	3,417	13,584	44,535	80,107	141,603	183,059	239,459
Texas	....	....	....	....	....	....	· 58,161
Vermont	17	....	....	....	....	....	....
Virginia	293,427	345,796	392,518	425,153	469,757	449,087	472,528
Wisconsin	....	....	....	....	....	11	....
TERRITORIES.							
Minnesota.....	....	....	....	....	....	....	....
New Mexico ...	....	....	....	....	....	....	....
Oregon........	....	....	....	....	....	....	....
Utah..........	....	....	....	....	....	....	26
				1,538,125 less 87			
Aggregate	697,897	893,041	1,191,364	1,538,038	2,009,043	2,487,455	3,204,313

14

TABLE V.

Increase and Decrease per cent of the Slave Population of the several States, at each Census.

States and Territories.	1800.	1810.	1820.	1830.	1840.	1850.
Alabama	....	....	.... *	* 180.68	* 115.68	* 35.22
Arkansas	....	....	....	* 182.99	* 335.64	* 136.26
Columbia, District of ...	....	* 66.30	* 18.20	† 4.04	† 23.28	† 21.45
Connecticut	† 65.53	† 67.40	† 68.70	† 74.22	† 32.00	....
Delaware	† 30.76	† 32.11	* 7.94	† 26.99	† 20.86	† 12.09
Florida	....	....	....	....	* 65.90	* 52.85
Georgia...............	* 102.99	* 77.12	* 42.23	* 45.35	* 29.15	* 35.85
Illinois	....	....	* 445.83	† 18.53	† 55.68	....
Indiana	....	* 75.55	† 19.83	† 98.42	....	....
Kentucky	* 241.02	* 99.69	* 57.31	* 30.36	* 10.31	* 15.75
Louisiana.............	....	....	* 99.26	* 58.67	* 53.71	* 45.32
Maryland	* 2.52	* 5.55	† 3.68	† 4.09	† 12.87	* .70
Mississippi	....	* 389.76	* 92.02	* 100.09	* 197.31	* 58.74
Missouri	....	....	* 239.48	* 145.46	* 132.11	* 50.10
New Hampshire	† 94.93	....	....	....	† 66.66	....
New Jersey	* 8.74	† 12.64	† 30.35	† 70.17	† 70.09	† 64.98
New York	† 4.60	† 26.18	† 32.82	† 99.25	† 94.66	....
North Carolina.........	* 32.53	* 26.65	* 21.43	* 19.79	* .08	* 17.38
Ohio	....	....	....	....	† 50.00	....
Pennsylvania	† 54.34	† 53.39	† 73.45	* 90.99	† 84.11	....
Rhode Island	† 59.97	† 71.65	† 55.55	† 64.58	† 70.58	....
South Carolina.........	* 36.46	* 34.35	* 31.62	* 22.02	* 3.68	* 17.71
Tennessee	* 297.54	* 227.84	* 79.87	* 76.76	* 29.27	* 30.80
Virginia	* 17.84	* 13.51	* 8.31	* 10.49	† 4.40	* 5.21

* Increase.   † Decrease.

TABLE VI.

Ratio of the Slave and total Colored Population to the total Population of each State.

States and Territories.	Slaves. 1790	1800	1810	1820	1830	1840	1850	Free Colored and Slaves. 1790	1800	1810	1820	1830	1840	1850
Alabama				32.7	37.9	42.9	44.4				33.1	38.4	43.2	44.7
Arkansas				11.3	15.0	20.4	22.4				11.8	15.5	20.9	22.7
California														1.0
Columbia, District of		23.0	22.4	19.3	15.3	10.7	7.1		28.5	33.0	31.5	30.8	29.8	26.5
Connecticut	1.1	.3	.1	.1				2.3	2.5	2.5	2.9	2.7	2.6	2.0
Delaware	15.0	9.5	5.7	6.2	4.2	3.3	2.5	21.6	22.4	23.8	24.0	24.9	25.0	22.2
Florida					44.6	47.2	44.9					47.0	48.7	46.0
Georgia	35.4	36.6	41.6	43.8	42.0	40.6	42.1	35.9	37.2	42.3	44.4	42.5	41.0	42.4
Illinois			1.3	.9	.4							.6	.8	.6
Indiana			.9	.1						2.5	2.5	1.0	1.0	1.1
Iowa						.1							.4	.1
Kentucky	16.1	18.2	19.8	22.4	24.0	23.3	21.4	16.3	18.5	20.2	22.9	24.7	24.3	22.5
Louisiana			45.2	45.0	50.8	47.8	47.2			55.4	52.1	58.5	55.0	50.6
Maine														.2
Maryland	32.2	30.9	29.3	26.3	23.0	19.0	15.5	34.7	36.6	38.2	36.1	34.8	32.3	28.3
Massachusetts								1.4	1.5	1.4	1.3	1.3	1.3	.9
Michigan			.5		.1					3.0		1.1	.3	.6
Mississippi		39.4	42.3	43.4	48.0	51.9	51.0		41.4	42.9	44.1	48.4	52.3	51.2
Missouri			14.4	15.8	17.8	15.1	12.8			17.3	15.9	18.2	15.5	13.2
New Hampshire	.1							.5	.4	.4	.3	.2	.1	.1
New Jersey	6.2	5.8	4.4	2.7	.7	.1		7.7	7.9	7.6	7.2	6.4	5.8	4.9
New York	6.2	3.4	1.5	.2				7.6	5.2	4.2	2.9	2.3	2.0	1.5
North Carolina	25.5	27.8	30.3	32.0	33.2	32.6	33.2	26.8	29.3	32.2	34.3	35.9	35.6	36.3
Ohio										.4	.8	1.0	1.1	1.2
Pennsylvania	.8	.2	.1					2.3	2.7	2.8	3.0	2.8	2.7	2.3
Rhode Island	1.3	.5						6.4	5.8	4.8	4.8	3.6	2.9	2.4
South Carolina	43.0	42.2	47.3	51.4	54.2	55.0	57.5	43.7	43.2	48.4	52.7	55.6	56.4	58.9
Tennessee	9.5	12.8	17.0	18.9	20.7	22.0	23.8	10.5	13.1	17.5	19.6	21.4	22.7	24.5
Texas							27.3							27.5
Vermont								.3	.3	.3	.3	.3	.2	.2
Virginia	39.2	39.2	40.2	39.9	38.7	36.2	33.2	40.9	41.5	43.4	43.3	42.6	40.2	37.0
Wisconsin														.2
Territories { Minnesota														.6
New Mexico														
Oregon							.2							1.5
Utah														.4

TABLE VII.

Classification of Slaveholders in the United States.

STATES, &c.	Holders of 1 slave	1 and under 5	5 and under 10	10 and under 20	20 and under 50	50 and under 100	100 and under 200	200 and under 300	300 and under 500	500 and under 1000	1000 and over	Aggregate holders of slaves
Alabama	5,204	7,737	6,572	5,067	3,524	957	216	16	2			29,295
Arkansas	1,383	1,951	1,365	788	382	109	19	2				5,999
Columbia, District of	760	539	186	89	2	1						1,477
Delaware	320	352	117	20								809
Florida	699	991	759	588	349	104	29		1			3,520
Georgia	6,554	11,716	7,701	6,499	5,056	764	147	22	4	2		38,456
Kentucky	9,244	13,284	9,579	5,022	1,198	53	5					38,385
Louisiana	4,797	6,072	4,327	2,652	1,774	728	274	36	6	4		20,670
Maryland	4,825	5,331	3,827	1,822	655	72	7		1			16,040
Mississippi	3,640	6,228	5,143	4,015	2,964	910	189	18	8	1		23,116
Missouri	5,762	6,878	4,370	1,810	345	19		1				19,185
North Carolina	1,204	9,668	8,129	5,898	2,828	485	76	12	3			28,303
South Carolina	3,492	6,164	6,311	4,955	3,200	990	382	69	29	2	2	25,596
Tennessee	7,616	10,582	8,314	4,852	2,202	276	19	2	1			33,864
Texas	1,935	2,640	1,585	1,121	374	82	9	1				7,747
Virginia	11,385	15,550	13,030	9,456	4,880	646	107	8	1			55,063
Total	68,820	105,683	80,765	54,595	29,733	6,196	1,479	187	56	9	2	347,525

TABLE VIII.

Farming Lands and Improvements, 1850.

AGRICULTURE.— The following table will show the relative number of farms, and quantity of acres in each, in the several States and Territories, as well as the value of farms and implements. The unimproved Land embraces such as is in occupancy and necessary to the enjoyment of the improved, though not itself reclaimed. Meadow lands, in all the States, are therefore regarded improved. The returns do not, however, distinguish always very clearly the improved from the unimproved.

14*

STATES.	Farms, Plantations, &c.	Acres of Improved Land	Acres of Unimproved Land	Average Number of Acres to each Farm.	Cash Value of Farms.	Value of Farming Implements and Machinery.	Average Value of Farms.	Average Value of Farming Implements and Machinery.	Average Value of Farms, Implements, and Machinery.
Alabama	41,964	4,435,614	7,702,067	289	$64,323,224	$5,125,663	$1,533	$122	$1,655
Arkansas	17,758	781,530	1,816,684	146	15,265,245	1,601,296	860	90	950
California	872	32,454	3,861,531	4,466	3,874,041	103,488	4,443	118	4,561
Columbia, District of	267	16,267	11,187	103	1,730,460	40,220	6,481	151	6,632
Connecticut	22,445	1,768,178	615,701	106	72,726,422	1,892,541	3,240	84	3,324
Delaware	6,063	580,862	375,282	158	18,880,081	510,279	3,114	84	3,198
Florida	4,304	349,049	1,246,240	371	6,323,109	658,795	1,469	153	1,622
Georgia	51,759	6,378,479	16,442,900	441	95,753,445	5,894,150	1,850	114	1,964
Illinois	76,208	5,039,545	6,997,867	158	96,133,290	6,405,561	1,261	84	1,345
Indiana	93,896	5,046,543	7,746,879	186	136,385,173	6,704,444	1,453	71	1,524
Iowa	14,805	824,682	1,911,382	185	16,657,567	1,172,869	1,125	79	1,204
Kentucky	74,777	5,968,270	10,981,478	227	155,021,262	5,169,037	2,073	69	2,142
Louisiana	13,422	1,590,025	3,399,018	372	75,814,398	11,576,938	5,648	863	6,511
Maine	46,760	2,039,596	2,515,797	97	54,861,748	2,284,557	1,173	49	1,222
Maryland	21,860	2,797,905	1,836,445	212	87,178,545	2,463,443	3,988	113	4,101
Massachusetts	34,069	2,133,436	1,222,576	99	109,076,347	3,209,584	3,202	94	3,296
Michigan	34,089	1,929,110	2,454,780	129	51,872,446	2,891,371	1,521	85	1,606

TABLE VIII.—Continued.

STATES AND TERRITORIES.	Farms, Plantations, &c.	Acres of Improved Land.	Acres of Unimproved Land.	Average Number of Acres to each Farm.	Cash Value of Farms.	Value of Farming Implements and Machinery.	Average Value of Farms.	Average Value of Farming Implements and Machinery.	Average Value of Farms, Implements, and Machinery.
Mississippi	33,960	3,444,358	7,046,061	309	$54,738,634	$5,762,927	$1,612	$170	$1,782
Missouri	54,458	2,938,425	6,794,245	179	63,225,543	3,981,525	1,161	73	1,234
New Hampshire	29,229	2,251,488	1,140,926	116	55,245,997	2,314,125	1,890	79	1,969
New Jersey	23,905	1,767,991	984,955	115	120,237,511	4,425,503	5,030	185	5,215
New York	170,621	12,408,964	6,710,120	113	554,546,642	22,084,926	3,250	129	3,379
North Carolina	56,963	5,453,975	15,543,008	369	67,891,766	3,931,532	1,192	69	1,261
Ohio	143,807	9,851,493	8,146,000	125	358,758,603	12,750,585	2,495	88	2,583
Pennsylvania	127,577	8,623,619	6,294,728	117	407,876,099	14,722,541	3,197	115	3,312
Rhode Island	5,385	356,487	197,451	103	17,070,802	497,201	3,170	92	3,262
South Carolina	29,967	4,072,551	12,145,049	541	82,431,684	4,136,354	2,751	138	2,889
Tennessee	72,735	5,175,173	13,808,849	261	97,851,212	5,360,210	1,345	74	1,419
Texas	12,198	643,976	10,852,363	942	16,550,008	2,151,704	1,357	176	1,533
Vermont	29,763	2,601,409	1,524,418	139	63,367,227	2,739,282	2,129	92	2,221
Virginia	77,013	10,360,135	15,792,176	340	216,401,543	7,021,772	2,810	91	2,901
Wisconsin	20,177	1,045,499	1,931,159	148	28,528,563	1,641,568	1,414	81	1,495
Territories. { Minnesota	157	5,035	23,846	184	1,653,922	15,981	1,031	102	1,133
New Mexico	3,750	166,201	124,370	77		77,960	441	21	462
Oregon	1,164	132,857	299,951	372	2,849,170	183,423	2,448	157	2,605
Utah	926	16,333	30,516	51	311,799	84,288	337	91	428
Total	1,449,075	113,032,614	180,528,000	203	3,271,575,426	151,587,638	2,258	105	2,362

The average number of acres embraced in each farm in the United States is 203, valued at $2,258, and upon each farm there is an average of $105 in implements and machinery. In Louisiana, so complicated is the sugar process, the average machinery is $863 to the farm.

LIVE STOCK AND AGRICULTURAL PRODUCTIONS. — The annexed table embraces the returns of agricultural products and live stock by the Census of 1840 and 1850. The quantity of wheat in 1850 is believed to be understated, and the crop was also short. Rough rice is returned for 1850, and clean rice for 1840. Corrections have been made in the cotton and sugar returns since the publication of the Quarto Census, pounds having been intended by the enumerators, in many cases, where they returned bales or hogsheads. It is impossible to reconcile the hemp and flax returns of 1840 and 1850. No doubt in both cases tons and pounds have often been confounded. In a few of the States, such as Indiana and Illinois, the returns of 1850 were rejected altogether for insufficiency. Letters from Kentucky, entitled to high credit, state the water-rotted hemp for that year to be not a third as much as the census gives, and the dew-rotted to be about 22,000 tons. In this case the whole hemp crop of 1850 may have reached 35,000 or 40,000 tons, and that of 1840, 25,000 to 30,000 tons.

TABLE IX.

Live Stock upon Farms, and Agricultural Productions, of the States and Territories, 1840 and 1850.

STATES.	Horses (1850)	Asses and Mules (1850)	Horses, Asses, and Mules (1850)	Horses and Mules (1840)	Milch Cows (1850)	Working Oxen (1850)	Other Cattle (1850)	Total Neat Cattle (1850)	Neat Cattle (1840)	Sheep (1850)	Sheep (1840)
Alabama	128,001	59,895	187,896	143,147	227,791	66,961	433,263	728,015	668,018	371,880	163,243
Arkansas	60,197	11,559	71,756	51,472	93,151	34,239	165,320	292,710	188,786	91,256	42,151
California	21,719	1,668	23,385		4,280	4,780	253,599	262,659		17,574	......
Columbia, District of	824	57	881	2,145	813	104	123	1,040	3,274	150	706
Connecticut	26,879	49	26,928	24,650	85,461	46,988	80,226	212,675	238,650	174,181	403,462
Delaware	13,852	791	14,643	14,421	19,248	9,797	24,166	53,211	53,883	27,503	39,247
Florida	10,848	5,002	15,850	12,043	72,876	5,794	182,415	261,085	118,081	23,311	7,198
Georgia	151,331	57,879	208,710	157,540	334,223	73,286	690,019	1,097,528	884,414	560,485	287,107
Illinois	267,653	10,573	278,226	199,235	294,671	76,156	541,209	912,036	626,274	894,043	395,672
Indiana	314,299	6,599	320,898	241,086	284,554	40,221	389,891	714,666	619,980	1,122,493	675,982
Iowa	38,536	754	39,290	10,794	45,704	21,892	69,025	136,621	38,049	149,960	15,354
Kentucky	315,682	65,609	381,291	395,853	247,475	62,274	442,768	752,512	787,098	1,102,091	1,008,240

TABLE IX.—Continued.

STATES AND TERRITORIES.	Horses. (1850)	Asses and Mules. (1850)	Horses, Asses, and Mules. (1850)	Horses and Mules. (1840)	Milch Cows. (1850)	Working Oxen. (1850)	Other Cattle. (1850)	Total Neat Cattle. (1850)	Neat Cattle. (1840)	Sheep. (1850)	Sheep. (1840)
Louisiana	89,514	44,849	134,363	99,888	105,576	54,968	414,798	575,342	381,248	110,333	98,072
Maine	41,721	55	41,776	59,208	133,556	83,893	125,890	343,339	327,255	451,577	649,264
Maryland	75,684	5,644	81,328	92,220	86,856	34,135	98,595	219,586	225,714	177,902	257,922
Massachusetts	42,216	34	42,250	61,484	130,099	46,611	83,484	259,994	282,574	188,651	378,226
Michigan	58,506	70	58,576	30,144	99,676	55,350	119,471	274,497	185,190	746,435	99,618
Mississippi	115,460	54,547	170,007	109,227	214,231	83,485	436,254	733,970	623,197	304,929	128,367
Missouri	225,319	41,667	266,986	196,032	230,169	112,168	449,173	791,510	433,875	762,511	348,018
New Hampshire	34,233	19	34,252	43,892	94,277	59,027	114,606	267,910	275,562	384,756	617,390
New Jersey	63,955	4,089	68,044	70,502	118,736	12,070	80,455	211,261	220,202	160,488	219,285
New York	447,014	963	447,977	474,543	931,324	178,909	767,406	1,877,639	1,911,244	3,453,241	5,118,777
North Carolina	148,693	25,259	173,952	166,608	221,799	37,309	434,402	693,510	617,371	595,249	538,279
Ohio	463,397	3,423	466,820	430,527	544,499	65,381	749,067	1,358,947	1,217,874	3,942,929	2,028,401
Pennsylvania	350,398	2,259	352,657	365,129	530,224	61,627	562,135	1,153,946	1,172,665	1,822,357	1,767,620
Rhode Island	6,168	1	6,169	8,024	18,698	8,139	9,375	36,262	36,891	44,296	90,146
South Carolina	97,171	37,488	134,654	129,921	193,244	20,507	563,935	777,686	572,660	285,551	232,981
Tennessee	270,636	75,303	345,939	341,409	250,456	86,255	414,051	750,762	822,851	811,591	741,593
Texas	76,760	12,463	89,223	.....	217,811	51,285	661,018	930,114	.....	100,530	.....
Vermont	61,057	218	61,275	62,402	146,128	48,577	154,143	348,848	834,341	1,014,122	1,681,819
Virginia	272,403	21,488	293,886	326,488	317,619	89,513	669,137	1,076,269	1,024,148	1,810,004	1,293,772
Wisconsin	30,179	156	30,335	5,735	64,339	42,801	76,293	183,433	30,269	124,896	8,462
Territories. { Minnesota	860	14	874	.....	607	655	740	2,002	.....	80	.....
New Mexico	5,079	8,654	13,733	.....	10,635	12,257	10,085	32,977	.....	877,271	.....
Oregon	8,046	420	8,466	.....	9,427	8,114	24,188	41,729	.....	15,382	.....
Utah	2,429	325	2,754	.....	4,861	5,266	2,469	12,616	.....	3,262	.....

TABLE IX. —*Continued.*

STATES.	Swine. 1850.	Swine. 1840.	Value of Live Stock. 1850.	Value of Animals Slaught'd. 1850.	Wheat, Bushels. 1850.	Wheat, Bushels. 1840.	Rye, Bushels. 1850.	Rye, Bushels. 1840.	Oats, Bushels. 1850.	Oats, Bushels. 1840.
Alabama	1,904,540	1,423,873	$21,690,112	$4,823,485	294,044	888,052	17,261	51,008	2,995,696	1,406,353
Arkansas	836,727	393,058	6,647,969	1,163,313	199,639	105,878	8,047	6,219	656,183	189,553
California	2,776		3,351,058	107,173	17,228					
Columbia, District of	1,635	4,673	71,648	9,088	17,370	12,147	5,509	5,081	8,185	15,751
Connecticut	76,472	181,961	7,467,490	2,202,266	41,762	87,009	600,893	737,424	1,258,738	1,453,262
Delaware	56,261	74,228	1,849,281	373,665	482,511	315,165	8,066	38,546	604,518	927,405
Florida	209,453	92,680	2,880,068	514,685	1,027	412	1,152	305	66,586	13,829
Georgia	2,168,617	1,457,755	25,728,416	6,389,762	1,088,534	1,801,830	53,750	60,693	3,820,044	1,610,030
Illinois	1,915,907	1,495,254	24,209,258	4,972,286	9,414,575	3,335,393	83,364	88,197	10,087,241	4,988,008
Indiana	2,263,776	1,623,608	22,478,555	6,567,985	6,214,458	4,049,375	78,792	129,621	5,655,014	5,981,605
Iowa	323,247	104,899	3,689,275	821,164	1,530,581	154,693	19,916	3,792	1,524,345	216,385
Kentucky	2,891,163	2,310,533	29,661,436	6,462,598	2,142,822	4,803,152	415,073	1,321,373	8,201,811	7,155,974
Louisiana	597,301	323,220	11,152,275	1,458,990	417	60	475	1,812	89,637	107,353
Maine	54,598	117,386	9,705,726	1,646,773	296,259	848,166	102,916	187,941	2,181,037	1,076,409
Maryland	352,911	416,943	7,997,634	1,954,800	4,494,680	3,345,783	226,014	723,577	2,242,151	3,534,211
Massachusetts	81,119	143,221	9,647,710	2,500,924	31,211	157,923	481,021	536,014	1,165,146	1,819,680
Michigan	205,847	295,890	8,008,734	1,328,327	4,925,889	2,157,108	105,871	84,236	2,866,056	2,114,051
Mississippi	1,582,734	1,001,209	19,403,662	3,636,582	137,990	196,626	9,606	11,444	1,503,288	668,624
Missouri	1,702,625	1,271,161	19,887,580	3,337,106	2,981,652	1,037,386	44,268	68,608	5,278,079	2,234,947
New Hampshire	63,487	121,671	8,871,901	1,522,873	185,658	422,124	183,117	308,148	973,381	1,296,114
New Jersey	250,370	261,443	10,679,291	2,633,552	1,601,190	774,203	1,255,578	1,665,820	3,378,063	3,053,524
New York	1,018,252	1,900,065	73,570,499	13,573,883	13,121,498	12,286,418	4,148,182	2,979,323	26,552,814	20,675,847
North Carolina	1,812,813	1,649,716	17,717,647	5,767,866	2,130,102	1,960,855	229,563	218,971	4,052,078	3,193,941
Ohio	1,964,770	2,099,746	44,121,741	7,439,243	14,487,351	16,571,631	425,918	814,205	13,472,742	14,393,103
Pennsylvania	1,040,366	1,503,964	41,500,053	8,219,848	15,367,691	13,213,077	1,805,160	6,613,873	21,538,156	20,641,819
Rhode Island	19,509	30,659	1,582,637	607,486	49	3,098	26,409	84,521	215,232	171,517
South Carolina	1,065,503	878,532	15,060,015	3,502,637	1,066,277	968,354	43,790	44,788	2,322,155	1,486,208
Tennessee	3,104,800	2,926,607	29,978,016	6,401,765	1,619,386	4,569,692	89,137	304,320	7,703,086	7,035,678

TABLE IX. — *Continued.*

STATES & TERRITORIES.	Oats, Bushels. 1850.	Oats, Bushels. 1840.	Rye, Bushels. 1850.	Rye, Bushels. 1840.	Wheat, Bushels. 1850.	Wheat, Bushels. 1840.	Value of Animals Slaught'd. 1850.	Value of Live Stock. 1850.	Swine. 1850.	Swine. 1840.
Texas	199,017		8,108		41,729		$1,116,187	$10,412,927	692,022	
Vermont	2,307,734	2,222,584	176,233	230,993	535,955	495,800	1,861,336	12,643,228	66,296	203,800
Virginia	10,179,144	13,451,062	458,930	1,482,799	11,212,616	10,109,716	7,502,986	33,656,659	1,829,843	1,992,155
Wisconsin	3,414,672	406,514	81,253	1,965	4,286,131	212,116	920,178	4,897,385	159,276	51,383
Territories { Minnesota	30,582		125		1,401		2,840	92,859	734	
New Mexico	5				196,516		82,125	1,494,629	7,314	
Oregon	61,214		106		211,943		164,530	1,876,189	30,235	
Utah }	10,900		210		107,702		67,985	543,968	914	

STATES.	Buckwheat, Bushels. 1850.	Buckwheat, Bushels. 1840.	Barley, Bushels. 1850.	Barley, Bushels. 1840.	Irish and Sweet Potatoes, Bushels. 1850. Irish.	Irish and Sweet Potatoes, Bushels. 1850. Sweet.	Irish and Sweet Potatoes, Bushels. 1850. Total.	Irish and Sweet Potatoes, Bushels. 1840. Irish and Sweet.	Indian Corn, Bushels. 1850.	Indian Corn, Bushels. 1840.
Alabama	348	58	3,958	7,692	246,001	5,475,204	5,721,205	1,708,356	28,754,048	20,947,004
Arkansas	175	88	177	760	193,882	788,149	981,981	293,608	8,893,939	4,846,632
California			9,712		9,292	1,000	10,292		12,236	
Columbia, District of	378	272	75	294	28,292	3,497	31,789	12,085	65,230	39,485
Connecticut	229,297	303,043	19,099	33,759	2,689,725	80	2,689,805	3,414,238	1,935,043	1,500,441
Delaware	8,615	11,299	56	5,260	240,542	65,443	305,985	200,712	3,145,542	2,069,359
Florida	55			30	7,828	757,226	765,054	264,617	1,996,809	898,974
Georgia	250	141	11,501	12,979	227,379	6,986,428	7,213,807	1,291,366	30,080,099	20,905,122
Illinois	184,504	57,884	110,795	82,251	2,514,861	157,433	2,672,294	2,025,520	57,646,984	22,634,211

TABLE IX. —*Continued.*

STATES & TERRITORIES	Indian Corn, Bushels. 1850.	1840.	Irish and Sweet Potatoes, Bushels. 1850. Irish.	1850. Sweet.	1850. Total.	1840. Irish and Sweet.	Barley, Bushels. 1850.	1840.	Buckwheat, Bushels. 1850.	1840.
Indiana	52,964,363	28,155,887	2,083,337	201,711	2,285,048	1,525,794	45,483	28,015	149,740	49,019
Iowa	8,656,799	1,406,241	276,120	6,243	282,363	284,063	25,093	728	52,516	6,212
Kentucky	58,672,591	39,847,120	1,492,487	998,179	2,490,666	1,055,085	95,343	17,491	16,097	8,169
Louisiana	10,266,373	5,952,911	95,632	1,428,453	1,524,085	834,341	......	......	3	......
Maine	1,750,056	950,528	3,436,040	......	3,436,040	10,392,280	151,731	355,161	104,523	51,543
Maryland	10,749,858	8,233,086	764,939	208,998	973,932	1,086,433	745	3,594	103,671	73,606
Massachusetts	2,345,490	1,809,192	3,585,384	......	3,585,384	5,885,652	112,385	165,319	105,895	87,000
Michigan	5,641,420	2,277,039	2,359,897	1,177	2,361,074	2,109,205	75,249	127,802	472,917	113,592
Mississippi	22,446,552	13,161,237	261,482	4,741,795	5,003,277	1,630,100	......	1,654	1,121	61
Missouri	36,214,537	17,332,524	939,006	335,505	1,274,511	788,768	9,631	9,801	23,641	15,818
New Hampshire	1,573,670	1,162,572	4,304,919	......	4,304,919	6,206,606	70,256	121,899	65,265	105,103
New Jersey	8,759,704	4,361,975	3,207,236	508,015	3,715,251	2,072,069	6,492	12,501	878,934	856,117
New York	17,858,400	10,972,286	15,398,368	5,629	15,403,997	30,123,614	3,585,059	2,520,008	3,188,955	2,287,885
North Carolina	27,941,051	23,893,763	620,318	5,095,092	5,716,027	2,609,239	2,735	3,574	16,704	15,394
Ohio	59,078,695	33,668,144	5,057,769	187,991	5,245,760	5,805,021	354,358	212,440	688,060	638,189
Pennsylvania	19,835,214	14,240,022	5,980,732	52,172	6,032,904	9,535,663	165,584	209,893	2,198,692	2,118,742
Rhode Island	539,201	450,498	651,029	......	651,029	911,973	18,875	63,490	1,245	2,979
South Carolina	16,271,454	14,722,805	136,494	4,337,469	4,473,960	2,698,313	4,583	3,907	283	72
Tennessee	52,276,223	44,986,188	1,067,844	2,777,716	3,845,560	1,904,370	2,737	4,809	19,427	17,118
Texas	6,028,876	......	94,645	1,332,158	1,426,803	......	4,776	......	59	......
Vermont	2,032,396	1,119,678	4,951,014	......	4,951,014	8,869,751	42,150	54,781	209,819	228,416
Virginia	35,254,319	34,577,591	1,316,383	1,813,634	3,130,567	2,944,660	25,487	87,490	214,898	248,822
Wisconsin	1,988,979	379,359	1,402,077	879	1,402,956	419,608	209,692	11,062	79,878	10,654
Territories { Minnesota	16,725	......	21,145	......	21,845	......	1,216	......	515	......
New Mexico	365,411	......	3	200	3	......	5	......	100	......
Oregon	2,918	......	91,326	......	91,326	......	......	......	......	......
Utah	9,899	......	43,968	60	44,028	......	1,799	......	332	......

TABLE IX.—Continued.

STATES.	Hay, Tons. 1850.	Hay, Tons. 1840.	Hops, Pounds. 1850.	Hops, Pounds. 1840.	Clover Seed. 1850.	Other Grass Seeds. 1850.	Butter and Cheese, lbs. 1850. Butter.	Butter and Cheese, lbs. 1850. Cheese.	Butter and Cheese, lbs. 1850. Total.	Dairy Products. 1840.	Peas and Beans. 1850.
Alabama	32,685	12,718	276	825	138	547	4,008,811	31,412	4,040,223	$265,200	892,701
Arkansas	8,976	586	157		90	436	1,854,239	30,088	1,884,327	59,205	285,738
California	2,088						705	150	855		2,292
Columbia, District of	2,279	1,331	15		3		14,872	1,500	16,872	5,566	7,754
Connecticut	516,181	426,704	554	28	13,841	16,628	6,498,119	5,363,277	11,861,396	1,376,534	19,090
Delaware	30,159	22,483	348	4,578	2,625	1,403	1,055,308	3,187	1,058,495	113,828	4,120
Florida	2,510	1,197	14	746		428	371,498	18,015	389,513	23,094	135,359
Georgia	23,449	16,970	261	773	132	2	4,640,559	46,976	4,687,585	605,172	1,142,011
Illinois	601,952	164,982	3,551	17,742	3,427	14,380	12,526,543	1,278,225	13,804,768	428,175	82,814
Indiana	403,230	178,029	92,796	38,591	18,320	11,951	12,881,535	624,664	13,506,099	742,269	35,773
Iowa	89,055	17,953	8,242	83	842	2,096	2,171,188	209,840	2,381,028	23,609	4,775
Kentucky	113,747	88,306	4,309	742	3,280	21,481	9,947,523	213,954	10,161,477	931,383	202,574
Louisiana	25,752	24,651	125	115		97	683,069	1,957	685,026	153,069	161,782
Maine	755,889	691,358	40,120	35,940	2	9,214	9,243,811	2,434,454	11,678,265	1,496,902	205,541
Maryland	157,956	106,687	1,870	2,357	9,097	2,561	3,806,160	3,975	3,810,185	457,466	12,816
Massachusetts	651,807	569,395	121,595	254,795	15,217	5,085	8,071,370	7,088,142	15,159,512	2,373,209	43,709
Michigan	404,934	130,805	10,663	11,381	16,989	9,295	7,065,878	1,011,492	8,077,870	301,052	74,254
Mississippi	12,504	171	473	154	84	533	4,346,234	21,191	4,367,425	359,585	1,072,757
Missouri	116,925	49,083	4,130	789	619	4,346	7,834,359	203,572	8,087,931	100,482	46,017
New Hampshire	598,854	496,107	257,174	243,425	829	8,071	6,977,056	3,196,563	10,173,619	1,688,543	70,856
New Jersey	435,950	384,861	2,183	4,531	28,280	63,051	9,487,210	365,756	9,852,966	1,328,082	14,174
New York	3,728,797	3,127,047	2,536,299	447,250	83,222	96,493	79,766,094	49,741,413	129,507,507	10,496,021	741,546
North Carolina	145,653	101,369	9,246	1,063	576	1,275	4,146,290	95,921	4,242,211	674,349	1,584,252
Ohio	1,443,142	1,022,037	68,781	62,195	108,197	37,310	34,449,379	20,819,542	55,268,921	1,848,869	60,168
Pennsylvania	1,842,970	1,311,643	22,088	49,481	125,030	53,913	39,878,418	2,505,084	42,383,452	3,187,292	55,281
Rhode Island	74,418	63,449	277	118	1,328	8,708	995,670	316,508	1,312,178	223,229	6,843
South Carolina	20,925	24,618	26	98	876	30	2,981,850	4,970	2,986,820	577,810	1,026,900
Tennessee	74,091	31,233	1,082	850	5,096	9,118	8,139,585	177,681	8,317,266	472,141	369,821

TABLE IX.—Continued.

States and Territories

States and Territories	Peas and Beans. 1850.	Dairy Products. 1840.	Butter and Cheese, lbs. 1850. Total.	Cheese. 1850.	Butter. 1850.	Other Grass Seeds. 1850.	Clover Seed. 1850.	Hops, Pounds. 1850.	Hops, Pounds. 1840.	Hay, Tons. 1850.	Hay, Tons. 1840.
Texas	179,350	....	2,440,199	95,299	2,344,900	....	10	7	....	8,354	....
Vermont	104,649	2,008,737	20,858,814	8,720,834	12,137,980	14,936	760	288,023	48,137	866,153	836,789
Virginia	521,579	1,490,488	11,525,651	436,292	11,089,359	23,428	29,727	11,506	10,597	869,098	364,708
Wisconsin	20,657	35,677	4,024,033	400,283	3,633,750	5,003	483	15,980	133	275,662	30,998
Territories { Minnesota	10,002	....	1,100	....	1,100	....	....	....	....	2,019	....
New Mexico	15,688	....	5,959	5,848	111	....	....	....	....	....	....
Oregon	6,566	....	248,444	36,980	211,464	22	4	8	....	873	....
Utah }	289	....	114,307	30,998	83,309	....	2	50	....	4,805	....

States

States.	Flaxseed bushels of. 1850.	Cords of Wood sold. 1840.	Home-made manufactures. Total. 1850.	Value of Poultry. 1840.	Wax, lbs. of. 1840.	Beeswax and Honey lbs. of. 1850.	Value of Orchard Products. 1840.	Value of Orchard Products. 1850.	Value of Nursery Products. 1850.	Value of Market Products. 1840.	Produce of Market Gardens. 1850.
Alabama	69	60,955	$1,984,120	$404,994	25,226	897,021	$55,240	$15,408	$370	$31,978	$84,821
Arkansas	321	78,606	688,217	109,468	7,079	192,388	10,680	40,141	415	2,736	17,150
California	....	....	7,000	....	....	....	....	17,700	....	....	75,275
Columbia, District of	....	1,287	2,075	3,092	44	550	3,507	14,843	850	52,895	67,222
Connecticut	703	159,062	192,252	176,629	3,897	93,804	296,232	175,118	18,114	61,936	196,874
Delaware	904	67,864	83,121	47,265	1,088	41,248	28,211	46,674	1,120	4,035	12,714
Florida	....	9,943	75,582	61,007	....	18,971	1,035	1,280	10	11,758	8,721
Georgia	622	57,459	1,838,968	449,623	19,799	782,514	156,122	92,776	1,853	19,846	76,500
Illinois	10,757	134,549	1,155,902	309,204	29,173	869,444	126,756	446,049	22,990	71,911	127,494

TABLE IX.—*Continued.*

STATES AND TERRITORIES.	Produce of Market Gardens. 1850.	Value of Market Products. 1840.	Value of Nursery Products. 1840.	Value of Orchard Products. 1850.	Value of Orchard Products. 1840.	Beeswax and Honey lbs. of. 1850.	Wax, lbs. of. 1840.	Value of Poultry. 1840.	Home-made manufactures. 1850.	Cords of Wood sold. 1840.	Flaxseed bushels of. 1850.
Indiana	$72,864	$61,212	$17,231	$324,940	$110,055	935,329	30,647	$357,694	$1,631,039	183,712	36,888
Iowa	8,848	2,170	4,200	8,494	50	821,711	2,182	16,529	221,292	7,304	1,959
Kentucky	303,120	125,071	6,226	106,230	484,935	1,158,019	83,445	536,439	2,459,128	264,222	75,801
Louisiana	148,329	240,042	32,415	22,359	11,769	96,701	1,012	288,559	189,232	202,867	.....
Maine	122,387	51,579	460	342,865	149,384	189,618	3,723	123,171	513,599	205,011	580
Maryland	200,869	138,197	10,591	164,051	105,740	74,802	3,674	218,765	111,828	178,181	2,446
Massachusetts	600,020	288,904	111,814	463,995	389,177	59,508	1,196	178,157	205,333	278,069	72
Michigan	14,738	4,051	6,307	132,650	16,075	359,232	4,533	82,730	340,947	54,498	519
Mississippi	46,250	42,896	499	50,405	14,458	897,460	6,885	369,482	1,164,020	118,423	26
Missouri	99,454	37,181	6,205	514,711	90,378	1,328,972	53,461	270,647	1,674,705	81,981	13,696
New Hampshire	56,810	18,085	-35	248,563	289,979	117,140	1,345	107,092	398,465	116,266	189
New Jersey	475,242	249,613	26,167	607,268	464,006	156,694	10,061	336,953	112,781	340,602	16,525
New York	912,047	499,126	75,980	1,761,950	1,701,093	1,755,830	52,795	1,153,413	1,280,383	1,058,923	57,963
North Carolina	39,462	28,475	48,681	34,348	386,006	512,289	118,923	544,125	2,086,522	40,034	38,196
Ohio	214,004	97,606	19,707	695,921	475,271	804,275	38,950	551,193	1,712,196	272,527	188,880
Pennsylvania	688,714	232,912	50,127	723,389	618,179	839,509	33,107	685,801	749,132	269,516	41,728
Rhode Island	98,298	67,741	12,604	63,994	32,098	6,347	165	61,702	26,495	48,666	.....
South Carolina	47,286	38,187	2,139	35,108	52,275	216,281	15,857	396,364	909,525	171,451	55
Tennessee	97,183	19,812	71,100	52,894	387,105	1,086,572	50,907	606,969	3,137,790	104,014	18,904
Texas	12,354			12,505		380,825			266,984		26
Vermont	18,853	16,276	5,600	315,255	213,944	249,422	4,660	131,578	267,710	96,899	989
Virginia	183,047	92,359	88,799	177,187	705,765	880,767	65,020	754,698	2,156,312	403,590	52,818
Wisconsin	32,142	8,106	1,025	4,823	87	131,005	1,474	16,167	43,624	22,910	1,191
Territories { Minnesota	150					80					
New Mexico	6,679			8,231		2			6,033		
Oregon	90,241			1,271							
Utah }	23,868					10			1,392		5

TABLE IX.—*Continued.*

STATES.	Flax, lbs. of.	Dew rt'd Hemp, tons.	W'r rt'd Hemp, tons.	Dew and wt'r rt'd Hemp, t's.	Hemp and Flax, tons.	Maple Sugar, lbs.	C'ne Sugar hhds. of 1000 lbs.	Molasses, galls. of.	Sugar, lbs. made.	G'd Cotton, bls. 400 lbs.	Cotton gathered, lbs. of.
	1850.	1850.	1850.	1850.	1840.	1850.	1850.	1850.	1840.	1840.	1840.
Alabama	3,921	....	....	....	5	643	87	83,428	10,143	564,429	117,138,823
Arkansas	12,291	....	15	15	1,039½	9,330	....	18	1,542	65,344	6,028,642
California	....	....	....	....	....	....	....	....	....	....	....
Columbia, Dist. of	....	....	....	....	....	....	....	....	....	....	....
Connecticut	17,928	....	....	....	41¾	50,796	....	665	51,764	....	....
Delaware	11,174	....	....	....	52¾	....	....	50	....	....	334
Florida	50	....	....	....	2	....	2,750	352,893	275,317	45,131	12,110,533
Georgia	5,387	....	....	....	10¾	50	846	216,245	329,744	499,091	163,392,396
Illinois	160,063	....	....	....	1,976¼	248,904	....	8,354	399,813	....	200,947
Indiana	584,469	....	....	....	8,605¼	2,921,192	....	180,325	3,727,795	14	180
Iowa	62,660	....	....	....	313¼	78,407	....	3,162	41,450	....	....
Kentucky	2,100,116	16,432	1,355	17,787	9,992¼	437,405	10	30,079	1,377,835	758	691,456
Louisiana	....	....	....	....	....	255	226,001	10,931,177	119,947,720	178,737	152,555,368
Maine	17,081	....	....	....	38	93,542	....	3,167	257,464	....	....
Maryland	35,686	63	....	63	488	47,740	....	1,430	36,266	....	5,673
Massachusetts	1,162	....	....	....	2¼	795,525	....	4,693	579,227	....	....
Michigan	7,152	....	....	....	755¼	2,439,794	....	19,823	1,329,784	....	....
Mississippi	665	7	....	7	16	....	8	18,318	77	484,292	193,401,577
Missouri	627,160	15,968	60	16,028	18,010¾	178,910	....	5,636	274,853	....	121,122
New Hampshire	7,652	....	....	....	26½	1,298,863	....	9,811	1,162,368	....	....
New Jersey	182,965	....	....	....	2,165¾	2,197	....	954	56	....	....
New York	940,577	1	3	4	1,130⅝	10,357,484	....	56,539	10,048,109	....	....
North Carolina	593,796	36	3	39	9,879¼	27,932	....	704	7,163	50,545	51,926,190
Ohio	446,932	100	50	150	9,080¼	4,588,209	....	197,308	6,363,386	....	....
Pennsylvania	530,307	44	....	44	2,649¾	2,326,525	....	50,652	2,265,755	....	....
Rhode Island	85	....	....	....	¼	28	....	4	50	....	....
South Carolina	333	....	....	....	....	200	77	15,904	30,000	300,901	61,710,274
Tennessee	368,131	454	141	595	3,344½	158,557	3	7,223	258,073	194,532	27,701,277

TABLE IX. — *Continued.*

STATES AND TERRITORIES.	Flax, lbs. of. 1850.	Dew rt'd Hemp, tons. 1850.	W'r rt'd Hemp, tons. 1850.	Dew and w't'r rt'd Hemp, t's. 1850.	Hemp and Flax, tons. 1840.	Maple Sugar, lbs. 1850.	Maple Sugar, lbs. 1840.	C'ne Sugar hhds. of 1000 lbs. 1850.	Molasses, galls. of. 1840.	Sugar, lbs. made. 1840.	G'd Cotton, bls. 400 lbs. 1840.	Cotton gathered, lbs. of. 1840.
Texas	1,048				.....		.....	7,351	441,918	.....	58,072	.....
Vermont	20,852				29¼		6,349,357		5,997	4,647,994		.....
Virginia	1,000,450	88	51	139	25,594½		1,227,665		40,322	1,541,833	3,947	3,494,483
Wisconsin	68,393				2		610,976		9,874	135,288		
TERRITORIES.												
Minnesota	.....						2,950					
New Mexico	640								4,236			
Oregon	550								24			
Utah	.....								58			

STATES.	Rough Rice, lbs. 1850.	Rice, lbs. 1850.	Rice, lbs. 1840.	Tobacco, lbs. 1850.	Tobacco, lbs. 1840.	Wool, lbs. 1850.	Wool, lbs. 1840.	Silk Cocoons, lbs. 1850.	Silk Cocoons, lbs. 1840.	Wine, galls. 1850.	Wine, galls. 1840.	Value of Family Goods. 1840.
Alabama	2,312,252		149,019	164,990	273,302	657,118	220,353	167	1,592¼	220	177	$1,656,119
Arkansas	63,179		5,454	218,936	148,439	182,595	64,943	88	95	35	.....	489,750
California				1,000		5,520				58,055	.....	
Columbia, District of				7,800	55,550	525	707	.....	651	863	25	1,500
Connecticut				1,267,624	471,657	497,454	889,870	328	17,588	4,269	2,636	226,162
Delaware				.....	272	57,768	64,404	.....	1,454¼	145	322	62,116
Florida	1,075,090		481,420	998,614	75,274	23,247	7,285	6	124¾	10	.....	20,205

TABLE IX.—*Continued.*

States and Territories	Rough Rice, lbs. 1850	Rice, lbs. 1840	Tobacco, lbs. 1850	Tobacco, lbs. 1840	Wool, lbs. 1850	Wool, lbs. 1840	Silk Cocoons, lbs. 1850	Silk Cocoons, lbs. 1840	Wine, galls. 1850	Wine, galls. 1840	Value of Family Goods. 1840
Georgia	38,950,691	12,384,732	423,924	162,894	990,019	371,303	813	2,992¼	796	8,647	$1,467,630
Illinois			841,394	564,826	2,150,113	650,007	47	1,150	2,997	474	993,567
Indiana			1,044,620	1,820,306	2,610,287	1,237,919	387	379	14,055	10,265	1,289,802
Iowa			6,041	8,076	373,898	23,039	246		420		25,966
Kentucky	5,688	16,376	55,501,196	53,436,909	2,297,433	1,786,847	1,281	737	8,093	2,209	2,622,462
Louisiana	4,425,349	3,604,534	26,878	119,284	109,897	49,283	29	317	15	2,884	65,190
Maine				80	1,364,034	1,465,551	252	211	724	2,236	804,397
Maryland			21,407,497	24,816,012	477,438	488,201	39	2,290¼	1,431	7,585	176,050
Massachusetts			138,246	64,955	585,136	941,906	7	1,741	498	193	231,942
Michigan			1,245	1,602	2,043,283	153,375	108	266	1,654		113,955
Mississippi			49,960	83,471	559,619	175,196	2	91	407	12	682,945
Missouri	2,719,856	777,195	17,113,784	9,067,913	1,627,164	562,265	186	70	10,563	22	1,149,544
New Hampshire	700	50	50	115	1,108,476	1,260,517	191	419¾	844	94	538,308
New Jersey			810	1,922	375,396	897,207	23	1,966	1,811	9,416	201,625
New York			83,189	744	10,071,301	9,845,295	1,774	1,785¼	9,172	6,799	4,636,547
North Carolina	5,465,868	2,820,388	11,984,786	16,772,359	970,738	625,044	229	3,014	11,058	28,752	1,413,242
Ohio			10,454,449	5,942,275	10,196,371	3,685,315	1,552	4,317¼	48,207	11,524	1,853,987
Pennsylvania			912,651	325,018	4,481,570	3,048,564	285	7,262¼	25,590	14,328	1,303,093
Rhode Island				817	129,692	188,830		458	1,013	803	51,150
South Carolina	159,980,613	60,590,861	74,285	51,519	487,233	299,170	123	2,080	5,880	643	930,703
Tennessee	258,854	7,977	20,148,932	29,550,432	1,364,378	1,060,332	1,923	1,217	92	653	2,886,661
Texas	88,203		66,897	535	131,917		22		99		
Vermont					3,400,717	3,699,235	208	4,286	659	94	674,548
Virginia	17,154	2,956	56,803,227	75,347,106	2,860,765	2,538,374	517	3,191	5,408	13,911	2,441,672
Wisconsin			1,268	115	253,963	6,777		½	113		12,567
Territories { Minnesota					85						
N. Mexico			8,467		32,901				2,363		
Oregon			325		29,686						
Utah			70		9,222						

TABLE X.

Agricultural Products of the United States — 1850 and 1840.

Agricultural Products.	1850.	1840.
Horses	4,886,719	4,335,669
Mules and Asses	559,331	} horses and
Horses, Asses, and Mules	4,896,050	mules.
Milch Cows	6,885,094	
Working Oxen	1,700,744	
Other Cattle	10,293,069	
Total Neat Cattle	18,878,907	14,971,586
Sheep	21,723,220	19,311,374
Swine	30,354,213	26,301,293
Value of Live Stock	$544,180,516	
Value of Animals slaughtered	$111,703,142	
Wheat, bushels	100,485,944	84,823,272
Rye, "	14,188,813	18,645,567
Oats, "	146,584,179	123,071,341
Indian Corn, bushels	592,071,104	377,531,875
Irish Potatoes, "	65,797,896	
Sweet Potatoes, "	38,268,148	108,298,060
Total "	104,066,044	
Barley, "	5,167,015	4,161,504
Buckwheat, "	8,956,912	7,291,743
Hay, tons	13,888,642	10,243,108
Hops, pounds	3,497,029	1,233,502
Clover Seed, bushels	468,978	
Other Grass Seeds, bushels	416,831	

Agricultural Products.	1850.	1840.
Butter, pounds	313,345,306	
Cheese, "	105,535,893	
Butter and Cheese, bushels	418,881,199	$33,787,008
Peas and Beans, bushels	9,219,901	
Market Gardens	$5,280,030	$2,601,196
Nursery Products, "		$593,534
Orchard "	$7,723,186	$7,256,904
Beeswax and Honey, pounds	14,853,790	Wax.. 628,303
Poultry		9,344,410
Family Goods	$27,493,644	$29,023,380
Cords of Wood		5,088,891
Flax Seed, Bushels	562,312	95,251 tons
Flax, pounds	7,709,676	} Hemp and Flax.
Dew Rotted Hemp, tons	33,193	
Water " "	1,678	
Maple Sugar, pounds	34,253,436	155,100,809
Sugar, Cane, hogsheads	237,133	} pounds.
Molasses, gallons	12,700,991	
Cotton, bales	2,445,793	1,976,198
Rice, pounds	215,313,497	80,841,422
Tobacco, "	199,752,655	219,163,319
Wool "	52,616,959	35,802,114
Silk Cocoons, pounds	10,843	61,652
Wine, gallons	221,249	124,734

TABLE XI.

Value of the Agricultural Products of the United States — 1850.

Products.	Value.	Products.	Value.
Indian Corn	$296,035,552	Flax	$770,967
Wheat	100,485,944	Wine	442,498
Cotton	98,603,720	Silk Cocoons	5,421
Hay	96,870,494	Live Stock, over one year old — annual product	175,000,000
Oats	43,975,253	Animals slaughtered	55,000,000
Butter	50,135,248	Poultry on the basis of 1840	13,000,000
Home-made Manufactures	27,493,644	Feathers	2,000,000
Potatoes, Irish	26,319,158	Milk, (not included in Butter and Cheese)	7,000,000
Potatoes, Sweet	19,134,074	Eggs	5,000,000
Wool	15,755,087	Cord Wood on the basis of 1840	20,000,000
Tobacco	13,982,686	Home-made Manufactures — one-half for Agricultural part. — *Tucker.*	13,746,822
Cane Sugar	12,378,850	Small Crops — basis of Rhode Island for Onions, Carrots, etc.	5,000,000
Rye	7,803,847	Residuum of Crops, not consumed by Stock, Corn Fodder, Cotton, Seed, Straw, Rice-Flour, and Manure. — *Patent Reports.*	100,000,000
Orchard Products	7,723,186	Cattle, Sheep, and Pigs, under one year old.	50,000,000
Buckwheat	6,969,838		$1,311,691,326
Peas and Beans	5,762,436		
Market Garden Products	5,280,030	Add for Orchard and Garden Products of cities, not included in above — Milk, Butter, Poultry, Horses, Cows, etc., in cities and towns.	15,000,000
Cheese	5,276,795		
Hemp	5,247,430		
Rice	4,000,000	Total Agricultural Products — 1849-50	$1,326,691,326
Barley	3,616,910	To which add for increase since 1850, and for the greater value of Agricultural Products, would give total for 1854.	1,600,000,000
Molasses	2,540,179		
Beeswax and Honey	2,876,606		
Clover Seed	2,344,890		
Maple Sugar	1,712,671		
Hops	1,223,960		
Flaxseed	843,468		
Grass Seeds (other than Clover)	833,662		

TABLE XII.

Product of Manufactures, Mining, and the Mechanic Arts — 1850.

States.	Individuals and establishm'ts.	Capital.	Raw Material used.	Hands Employed. Male.	Female.	Annual Wages.	Annual Product.	Per cent Profit.
Alabama.............	1,026	$3,450,606	$2,224,960	4,399	539	$1,106,112	$4,528,878	34.71
Arkansas............	272	324,065	268,564	873	30	169,856	607,436	52.81
California...........	1,003	1,006,197	1,201,154	3,964	.....	3,485,820	12,862,522	812.52
Columbia, District of..	395	888,965	1,339,146	1,678	498	616,152	2,498,008	60.49
Connecticut.........	3,482	23,890,348	23,589,397	31,287	16,483	11,695,236	45,110,102	41.13
Delaware............	531	2,978,945	2,864,607	3,237	651	936,924	4,649,296	28.46
Florida.............	103	547,060	220,611	876	115	199,452	668,385	45.88
Georgia.............	1,527	5,460,483	3,404,917	660	1,718	1,712,304	7,086,525	36.06
Illinois.............	3,164	6,385,387	8,915,173	11,632	433	3,286,249	17,236,073	78.85
Indiana.............	4,288	7,941,602	10,214,337	13,677	665	2,809,116	18,922,651	74.28
Iowa...............	522	1,292,875	2,356,881	1,687	20	473,016	3,551,783	55.83
Kentucky............	3,609	12,350,734	12,170,225	22,445	1,940	4,764,096	24,588,483	61.97
Louisiana...........	1,017	5,318,074	2,958,988	5,551	856	2,086,212	7,320,948	42.79
Maine..............	3,977	14,700,452	13,555,806	21,856	6,222	7,502,916	24,664,136	24.52
Maryland...........	3,259	14,753,143	17,826,734	22,641	7,483	7,374,672	32,477,702	52.71
Massachusetts.......	8,259	83,357,642	85,856,771	96,261	69,677	39,784,116	151,137,145	30.59
Michigan...........	1,963	6,534,250	6,105,561	8,980	960	2,387,928	10,976,894	38.01
Mississippi.........	877	1,833,420	1,290,271	8,065	108	775,128	2,972,088	49.45
Missouri............	3,029	9,079,695	12,446,788	15,977	873	3,184,764	23,749,265	89.41
New Hampshire......	3,211	18,242,114	12,745,466	14,103	12,989	6,123,876	23,164,503	23.55
New Jersey..........	4,108	22,184,730	21,992,186	28,549	8,762	9,202,788	39,713,586	38.40
New York...........	23,553	99,904,405	134,655,674	147,737	51,612	49,131,000	237,597,249	53.86
North Carolina......	2,604	7,252,225	4,805,463	10,693	1,751	1,796,748	9,111,245	34.60
Ohio...............	10,622	29,019,538	34,677,987	47,064	4,435	13,467,660	62,647,259	49.97
Pennsylvania........	21,605	94,473,810	87,206,377	124,688	22,078	37,163,232	115,044,910	22.47
Rhode Island........	853	12,923,176	18,183,889	12,837	8,044	5,006,656	22,093,258	30.18
South Carolina......	1,431	6,056,865	2,809,554	6,985	1,074	1,128,482	7,063,513	51.60

TABLE XII. — Concluded.

Product of Manufactures, Mining, and the Mechanic Arts — 1850.

STATES.	Individuals and establishm'ts.	Capital.	Raw Material used.	Hands Employed. Male.	Female.	Annual Wages.	Annual Product.	Per cent Profit.
Tennessee	2,861	6,975,275	4,900,952	11,154	878	2,277,228	9,728,438	36.56
Texas	309	539,290	394,642	1,042	24	322,368	1,165,538	83.17
Vermont	1,849	5,001,377	4,172,552	6,894	1,551	2,202,848	8,570,920	43.91
Virginia	4,741	18,109,993	18,108,483	28,789	3,820	5,413,764	29,705,387	34.17
Wisconsin	1,262	3,382,148	5,414,931	5,798	291	1,712,496	9,293,068	64.00
TERRITORIES.								
Minnesota	5	94,000	24,000	63		21,420	57,500	12.85
New Mexico	23	68,300	110,220	81	32	20,772	249,010	172.79
Oregon	52	843,600	809,560	285		388,620	2,236,640	123.10
Utah	14	44,400	337,381	51		5,400	291,220	
Total	121,855	$527,209,193	$554,655,058	719,479	225,512	$229,736,377	$1,013,336,463	43.43

TABLE XIII.

Real and Personal Estate — 1850.

STATES & TERRITORIES.	Real Estate.	Personal Estate.	Total.	True Valuation.
Alabama..............	$78,870,718	$162,463,705	$241,334,423	$228,204,332
Arkansas.............	17,372,524	19,056,151	36,428,675	39,841,025
California	16,347,442	5,575,731	21,923,173	22,161,872
Columbia, District of ..	14,409,413	1,774,342	16,183,755	16,723,619
Connecticut	96,412,947	22,675,725	119,088,672	155,707,980
Delaware ....·....	14,486,595	1,410,275	15,896,870	18,855,863
Florida	7,924,588	15,274,146	23,198,734	23,198,734
Georgia	121,619,739	213,490,486	335,110,225	335,425,714
Illinois...............	81,524,835	33,257,810	114,782,645	156,265,006
Indiana	112,947,740	39,922,659	152,870,399	202,650,264
Iowa	15,672,332	6,018,310	21,690,642	23,714,638
Kentucky.............	177,013,407	114,374,147	291,387,554	301,628,456
Louisiana	176,623,654	49,832,464	226,456,118	233,998,764
Maine.	64,336,119	32,463,434	96,799,553	122,777,571
Maryland.............	139,026,610	69,536,956	208,563,566	219,217,364
Massachusetts........	349,129,932	201,976,892	551,106,824	573,342,286
Michigan.............	25,580,371	5,296,852	30,877,223	59,787,255
Mississippi	65,171,438	143,250,729	208,422,167	228,951,130
Missouri.............	66,802,223	31,793,240	98,595,463	137,247,707
New Hampshire.......	67,839,108	27,412,488	95,251,596	103,652,835
New Jersey .....,.....	153,151,619	Not returned.	153,151,619	153,151,619
New York............	564,649,649	150,719,379	715,369,028	1,080,309,216
North Carolina.......	71,702,740	140,368,673	212,071,413	226,800,472
Ohio.................	337,521,075	96,351,557	433,872,632	504,726,120
Pennsylvania	427,865,660	72,410,191	500,275,851	729,144,998
Rhode Island.........	54,358,231	23,400,743	77,758,974	80,508,794
South Carolina.......	105,737,492	178,130,217	283,867,709	288,257,694
Tennessee	107,981,793	87,299,565	195,281,358	207,454,704
Texas................	28,149,671	25,414,000	53,563,671	55,362,340
Vermont	57,320,369	15,660,114	72,980,483	92,205,049
Virginia..............	252,105,824	130,198,429	382,304,253	391,646,438
Wisconsin	22,458,442	4,257,083	26,715,525	42,056,595
Terri- / Minnesota	97,363	164,725	262,088	262,088
tories \ New Mexico...	2,679,486	2,494,985	5,174,471	5,274,867
\ Oregon..,......	3,997,332	1,066,142	5,063,474	5,063,474
\ Utah..........	337,866	648,217	986,083	986,083
Total.............	$3,899,226,347	$2,125,440,562	$6,024,666,909	$7,066,562,966

TABLE XIV.

Annual Taxes.

STATES.	ANNUAL TAXES.			
	State.	County.	School.	Road.
Alabama..............................	$428,690	$202,960	$7,519	$3,000
Connecticut...........................	67,947	1,101	48,669	80,117
Florida...............................	58,616	23,690	105	....
Georgia...............................	292,707	156,061	15,728	1,388
Indiana....⸱..........................	552,463	449,616	96,736	171,554
Maine................................	381,911	141,705	234,842	563,887
Mississippi...........................	779,163	436,993	31,106	4,698
New Hampshire	77,313	84,854	144,178	250,913
New Jersey	....	190,685	62,706	119,614
New York.............................	....	....	....	....
North Carolina.......................	114,086	144,189	42,340	660
Pennsylvania	1,536,662	1,689,212	840,066	816,867
Rhode Island........................⸳.	16,951	....	56,937	29,077
South Carolina.......................	373,421	....	....	20,817
Texas................................	74,936	35,055	....	....
Vermont..............................	138,533	3,578	88,930	247,801
Virginia..............................	268,649	229,285	45,697	20,309
Wisconsin	93,982	151,835	75,980	72,103
Total.............................	....	....	....	....

TABLE XV.

CALIFORNIA STATE CENSUS, 1852.

Agriculture and Manufactures.

The aggregates of productions of Agriculture and Manufactures for California, as given by the Secretary of State, are as follows:

Productions and Capital of the State.		Productions and Capital of the State.	
Number of Horses	64,773	Bushels of Corn	62,532
Number of Mules	16,578	Acres of Land under cultivation	110,748
Number of Cows	104,390	Number of Quartz Mills	108
Number of Beef Cattle	315,392	Capital invested in —	
Number of Working Oxen	29,065	Quartz Mining	$5,871,405
Bushels of Barley	2,973,734	Placer Mining	4,174,419
Bushels of Oats	100,497	Other Mining operations	3,851,623
Bushels of Wheat	271,763	For other purposes	41,061,933
Bushels of Potatoes	1,393,170		

PRODUCTIONS OF AGRICULTURE, 1852.

[From Andrews' Report on Lake Commerce. This Table is referred to in the text.]

The subjoined Table is designed to exhibit a general view of the Agriculture of the United States. The aggregate quantity and value of crops are first presented, and next the several items which are supposed to constitute the fixed capital of the Agricultural interest. It has been thought proper to assign one-fourth of the value of live stock to the column of annual production, as that is probably the rate of yearly increase. The remainder, together with the value of farms and farming implements and machinery, should obviously be reckoned as capital. In ascertaining the average price of crops, those of the New York Price Current for January, 1853, have been taken, and a deduction therefrom of fifteen per cent has been made, to cover expenses of transportation and commercial charges. Where special circumstances require a departure from this rule, they are noticed in the remarks appended to the Table.

TABLE. XVI.

Table showing the amount and value of the productions of Agriculture in the United States for the year 1852.

Productions.	Quantity.	Price.	Total value.
Wheat, bushels......................	143,000,000	$1 00 pr bush	$143,000,000
Rye, bushels........................	15,607,000	89 "	13,880,230
Indian Corn, bushels................	652,000,000	60 "	391,200,000
Oats, bushels.......................	161,000,000	44 "	70,840,000
Rice, pounds........................	236,843,000	034 pr lb.	8,052,662
Tobacco, pounds.....................	283,000,000	06 "	16,980,000
Cotton, pounds......................	1,290,000,000	10 "	129,000,000
Wool, pounds.......................	58,067,000	50 "	29,033,500
Peas and Beans, bushels.............	10,141,000	80 pr bush	8,112,800
Irish Potatoes, bushels..............	97,500,000	75 "	73,125,000
Sweet Potatoes, bushels.............	42,085,000	80 "	33,668,000
Barley, bushels.....................	5,683,000	60 "	3,409,800
Buckwheat, bushels.................	9,900,000	50 "	4,950,000
Orchard Produce....................	....	....	10,000,000
Wine, gallons......................	1,000,000	50 per gall.	500,000
Value of Produce of Market Gardens...	....	....	50,000,000
Butter, pounds.....................	344,592,000	20 per lb.	68,918,400
Cheese, pounds.....................	116,088,000	06 "	6,964,280
Hay, tons..........................	15,222,000	12 50 per ton.	190,275,000
Clover and other Grass Seeds, bushels..	974,380	5 00 pr bush	4,871,900
Flax Seed, bushels..................	8,487,500	1 30 "	11,033,750
Hops, pounds.......................	4,231,000	17 per lb.	719,270
Hemp, tons........................	39,000	136 00 per ton.	5,304,000
Flax, pounds.......................	15,420,000	06 per lb.	925,200
Maple Sugar, pounds................	39,675,000	05 "	1,983,750
Cane Sugar, pounds.................	272,339,000	04 "	10,893,000
Molasses, gallons...................	13,970,000	25 per gall.	3,442,500
Beeswax and Honey, pounds..........	16,500,000	20 per lb.	3,750,000
Animals slaughtered.................	....	....	133,000,000
Poultry............................	....	....	20,000,000
Feathers...........................	....	....	2,000,000
Milk and Eggs......................	....	....	25,000,000
Residuum of crops not consumed by stock..............................	....	....	110,000,000
Annual increase of Live stock........	....	....	167,750,000
Total annual productions of Agriculture	....	....	$1,752,583,042

16

VOTE FOR PRESIDENT, 1856.

THE following is the vote for President at the late Presidential Election, as given in the New York Tribune of December 19, 1856, which says the votes of the several States are nearly all official. The vote of California is taken from a later number of the Tribune. The scattering votes, and votes not returned in season to be officially counted, are not included. The estimate of the Tribune for South Carolina is a large one.

TABLE XVII.

Free States.	Buchanan.	Fremont.	Fillmore.
Maine.................................	38,035	65,514	3,233
New Hampshire.........................	32,567	38,158	414
Vermont...............................	10,577	39,561	511
Massachusetts	39,240	108,190	19,626
Rhode Island..........................	6,680	11,467	1,675
Connecticut...........................	34,995	42,715	2,615
New York	195,878	274,705	124,604
New Jersey	46,943	28,351	24,115
Pennsylvania	230,154	147,350	82,178
Ohio..................................	170,874	187,497	28,125
Michigan	52,139	71,062	1,567
Indiana...............................	118,672	94,816	23,386
Illinois.............................	104,279	96,280	37,451
Wisconsin.............................	52,867	66,092	579
Iowa	36,241	44,127	9,444
California............................	51,925	20,339	35,113
Total.............	1,221,846	1,336,914	394,629

Thus, the popular vote in the Free States was:

Fremont... 1,336,914
Buchanan.. 1,221,836
Fillmore.. 394,629
                                                          ──────────
Total vote in Free States................................ 2,953,379

TABLE XVII. — *Continued.*

Slave States.	Buchanan.	Fillmore.	Fremont.
Delaware	8,003	6,175	306
Maryland..............................	39,115	47,462	281
Virginia...............................	89,975	60,039	291
North Carolina........................	48,246	36,886	....
South Carolina *......................	30,000	20,000	....
Georgia...............................	56,617	42,372	....
Florida	6,368	4,843	....
Alabama	46,817	28,557	....
Mississippi............................	35,665	24,490	....
Louisiana.............................	22,169	20,709	....
Texas.................................	28,757	15,244	....
Arkansas..............................	21,908	10,816	....
Tennessee	73,638	66,178	....
Kentucky	72,917	65,822	369
Missouri..............................	58,164	48,524	....
Total..................................	638,359	498,117	1,247

* Estimated.

Thus, the popular vote of the Slave States was:

Buchanan..	638,359
Fillmore...	498,117
Fremont...	1,247
Total vote in Slave States..............................	1,137,723

RECAPITULATION.

Names.	Free States.	Slave States.	Total.	Electors.
Fremont.........................	1,336,914	1,247	1,338,161	114
Buchanan.......................	1,221,846	638,359	1,860,205	174
Fillmore.........................	394,629	498,117	892,746	8
Total....	2,953,389	1,137,723	4,091,112	296

TABLE XVIII.

Statistics of Iowa in 1856.

THE following extract from the Message of Gov. Grimes, to the Legislature of Iowa, gives the Statistics of that State according to a Census taken in June, 1856. The Governor's Message is dated Dec. 2, 1856:

An enumeration of the inhabitants of the State, and of her productive resources, was taken in June last, as required by the Constitution. It is somewhat defective — two counties and several townships in other counties not having been returned at all, while in almost all the counties there are very great omissions. Many townships and some counties are returned without any statistics, save those in relation to population.

The Census Returns show that the State has increased in population from June, 1854, to June, 1856, from 326,014 to 503,625.

The following statement will show the increase of population since the settlement of what is now the State:

1836	10,531	1847	116,204
1838	22,859	1849	130,945
1840	43,116	1850	192,204
1844	71,650	1854	326,014
1846	78,988	1856	503,625

The population of the State is probably at this time not far from 600,000. The vote polled on the 4th day of November last reached 92,644, and indicates the truth of this supposition.

The following Table shows the annual increase of the value of assessable property in the State, during the past six years:

1851 the assessable value was..	$28,464,550	1854 the assessable value was.. $72,327,204
1852 " " " "	33,427,876	1855 " " " " 106,895,390
1853 " " " "	49,540,304	1856 " " " " 164,194,413

As the Census Returns may not be published before your limited session will expire, I present a summary of some of the most important facts disclosed by it:

No. of Dwellings in the State in June last.	83,455
" Families in the State " "	89,161
" White male persons " "	267,929
" White female persons " "	235,425
" Colored persons " "	271
" Married persons " "	169,312
" Widowed persons " "	10,997
" Native voters " "	86,781
" Naturalized voters " "	14,456
" Aliens " "	15,104
" Militia " "	92,262
" Deaf and dumb " "	371
" Blind " "	102
" Insane " "	120
" Idiotic " "	257
" Owners of land " "	66,716
" Paupers	132
" Acres of improved land " "	2,342,958
" Acres of unimpr'd land " "	6,483,871
" Acres of meadow land " "	140,242
" Tons of Hay produced in 1855.	223,233
" Bushels Grass Seed harvested in 1855.	20,789
" Acres Spring Wheat in 1855.	345,518
" Bushels harvested in 1855.	4,972,639
" Acres of Winter Wheat in 1855.	41,034
" Bushels harvested in 1855.	495,703
" Acres of Oats in 1855.	190,158

No. of Bushels harvested in 1855	6,054,341
" Acres of Corn in 1855	732,803
" Bushels harvested in 1855	30,985,127
" Acres of Potatoes in 1855	180,041
" Bushels harvested in 1855	2,013,408
" Hogs sold in 1855	402,676
Value of Hogs sold in 1855	$3,119,378
No. of Cattle sold in 1855	125,000
Value of Cattle sold in 1855	$2,904,563
No. of pounds of Butter made in 1855	6,075,739
" " Cheese " "	729,852
" " Wool produced in 1855	515,808
Value of Domestic Manufactures in 1855	$438,322
" General Manufactures in 1855	$4,684,461
" Lead produced in 1855	$213,000

NOTE. — In Table X., page 31, there is an error in the column of value of Farm Implements and Machinery, in regard to the States of Kentucky and Louisiana; and, consequently, in the footing of that column. The reader can readily correct the error by referring to the original Table in the Appendix.

INDEX.

AGRICULTURE.

(187)

COMMERCE.

EDUCATION.

POPULAR REPRESENTATION.

POPULATION.